Live & Learn

PERSPECTIVES ON THE QUESTING SPIRIT

Live & Learn

PERSPECTIVES ON THE QUESTING SPIRIT

Edited by Carol S. Lawson & Robert F. Lawson

CHRYSALIS BOOKS / *Swedenborg Foundation Publishers*
West Chester, Pennsylvania

THE CHRYSALIS READER is a book series that examines themes related to the universal quest for wisdom. Inspired by the Swedenborg Foundation journal *Chrysalis,* each volume presents original short stories, essays, poetry, and art exploring the spiritual dimensions of a chosen theme. Works are selected by the series editors. For information on future themes or submission of original writings, contact Carol S. Lawson, Route 1, Box 184, Dillwyn, Virginia 23936.

© 2001 by the Swedenborg Foundation

Printed on recycled paper and bound in the United States of America.

LIBRARY OF CONGRESS CATALOGING-IN-PUBLICATION DATA
Live & learn : perspectives on the questing spirit / edited by Carol S. Lawson & Robert F. Lawson.
p. cm. — (Chrysalis reader ; v. 8)
ISBN 0-87785-232-4
1. Education—Literary collections. 2. American literature—20th century.
I. Title: Live and learn. II. Lawson, Carol S. III. Lawson, Robert F., 1948–
IV. Series
PS509.E36 L58 2001
810.8´0355—dc21

2001042372

 **CHRYSALIS BOOKS**

Swedenborg Foundation Publishers
320 North Church Street
West Chester, Pennsylvania 19380

Marc Chagall. *En Avant*. Gouache on paper, 48.9×38.1 cm., 1917. Art Gallery of Ontario, Toronto. Gift of Sam and Ayala Zacks, 1970. 2001 Artists Rights Society (ARS), New York, ADAGP, Paris.

Contents

EDITOR'S NOTE
A Boatload of Knowledge ix
   Robert F. Lawson

PREFACE
In Search of the Miraculous xi
   Robert Masters

PART I: THE SPIRIT ADVENTUROUS
   Florida (poem)
I've Got It! xiii
   Ray Silverman
Meeting Virginia Woolf at the Station 8
   Ruth Latta

"Let Me Show You How It Works" 13
    Ralph E. Pray

Child Therapy (poem) 18
    Alan Pucciarello

The Student You Can't Set on Fire 19
    Heather Heilman

Playing with Heart 23
    Richard C. Collins

The Writing Teacher (poem) 28
    Lynn Valente

Victorian Home Schooling: Frank Sewall Educates His Daughters . 29
    Alice Archer Sewall James

PART II: LEARNING STYLES
    Climbing Trees (poem)

When Birds Meet Again 41
    M. Garrett Bauman

Suffer Fools Gladly 46
    Don Rose and Mike Taylor

Most Poets Draw (poem) 54
    Errol Miller

Juggling Your Smarts 55
    Robert M. Peck

Exchange Student: Middle-School Teachers
Educate an Academic Physician 61
    Michael J. Lichtenstein

Europa (poem) 68
    Stuart Arotsky

Body Surfing 70
    Heather Taylor

The Opened "I" 74
    Andrew Flaxman

Husband Number One 79
    Loraine Campbell

PART III: SCHOOL DAYS
    The Whale Race (poem)

"New-Church" Education 85
    Naomi Gladish Smith

My Topographical Map of France (fiction) 92
    Lani Wright

Creative Writing (poem) 95
    Carol Lem

Scapegoat 97
    Andrea Rogers

Grades as Zen Koans 101
    Robert H. Herzog

Blind Typing (poem) 106
   Eleanora Patterson
The Game (fiction) 108
   John A. Conroy

PART IV: MENTORING
   Mountain Men (poem)
The Tender Intent 117
   Terry Marotta
The Game (poem) 122
   Thomas R. Smith
Learning a New Language 125
   Laura Lawson Tucker
Why My Grandfather Didn't Play for the New York Yankees (fiction) 129
   David D. Jones
Alan's Choice 135
   Marjorie Anderson
The Mind–Body Problem or My Dog Skippy (poem) 139
   Neal Weiner
At the Bedside 141
   Walter R. Christie

PART V: BEYOND THE CLASSROOM
   Vacations (poem)
Dining with the Dos Passos: A Lesson in Hospitality 149
   Rosalind Baker Wilson
The Education of William Page: Painting Soul into Canvas
and America's Entry into Modern Art 153
   Dino Adkins
In Movies, Blond and Thin Is Best (poem) 162
   Marian Charles
One Hour (fiction) 164
   Thomas F. Williams
Stuffed (fiction) 171
   Joe Lunievicz
Lessons Learned from a Sanitized America 175
   Don Kissil
When Spirit Moves 181
   Lorraine Sando
Offerings (poem) 186
   Corrine De Winter
A Thirst for Meaning 188
   Wanda Luttrell
Up from Bed 194
   Leatrice Johnson

A Boatload
of Knowledge

THIS CHRYSALIS READER IS OUR EDUCATION ISSUE—not that every issue hasn't been in its own unique way an education for our staff. However, this issue is specifically about the living and learning process—how the two are inseparable. Rather than recap the contents of each part of *Live & Learn,* we thought it might provide insight to the editors' predilictions to look at an extraordinary event that occurred on the American frontier when our country was not quite fifty years old.

In winter 1825, wealthy British industrialist Robert Owen brought reinforcements to his fledgling experiment of communal living at New Harmony—a small utopian community near the mouth of the Wabash River in Indiana. The reinforcements were intellectuals, scientists, and educators who had come down the Ohio River with their books, scientific equipment, and other paraphernalia in the *Philanthropist*—a keel boat contemporaries quickly dubbed the "boatload of knowledge." Among the passengers were Owen's son Robert Dale Owen, an educator, along with artists, geologists, a chemist, architect, civil engineer, naturalist, and several other educators and social reformers. At Louisville, educator Joseph Neef met the group and promised to sell his farm and join them later that winter.[1]

This adventurous group joined forces with over a thousand Owenites at New Harmony. Their goal was lofty—to bring into the light a new order for society, an enlightened social system based on equality that would eventually "bring great comfort and peace to all humanity." Owen was adept at public relations, and wherever he traveled in America, he utilized his oratory and communication skills to promote his venture. He met President John Quincy Adams, members of the Supreme Court, senators, and twice spoke before Congress. Through newspaper advertisements, public meetings, private consultations with influential businessmen and statesmen, New Harmony was attracting an interesting cross-section of humanity—professionals, skilled laborers, and an assortment of cranks, misfits, and ne'er-do-wells. Recruiting as he descended the Ohio, Owen lectured in Pittsburgh and Cincinnati. The latter city was at that time the center for Swedenborgian activities in the Midwest, and it was here that Owen became acquainted with the followers of the writings of Swedenborg. These congenial, intelligent, and educated people may have seen in Owen's social enterprise the seeds of Swedenborg's Universal Man: a vision of humankind living in separate and unique communities, yet functioning as an organic whole, a divine pattern that thrives on diversity.

Under the leadership of Daniel Roe, one of the Swedenborgian lay preachers, many of the Cincinnati congregation with others of the city and surrounding area purchased a site in Yellow Springs (present-day location of Antioch University) and established a village of 75 to 100 families under the Owenite principle of absolute democracy. According to one source:

> Men who seldom or never before labored with their hands, devoted themselves to agriculture and the mechanical arts with a zeal which was at least commendable, though not always according to knowledge. Ministers of the Gospel guided the plough, called the swine to their corn instead of sinners to repentance, and let patience have her perfect work over an unruly pair of oxen. Merchants exchanged the yard stick for the rake and pitchfork, and all appeared to labor cheerfully for the common weal. Among the women, there was even more apparent self-sacrifice. Ladies who had seldom seen the inside of their own kitchens, went into that of the common eating house, formerly a hotel, and made themselves useful among the pots and kettles; and refined young ladies, who had all their lives been waited upon, took their turns in waiting upon others at table. And several times a week, all parties who chose, mingled in the social dance in the great dining hall.[2]

In the end, the Yellow Springs group fell apart, obviously due in part to the complexities of cooperative living. The suppressed needs of individuals eventually came to the surface, and people found themselves living in a hellish situation. Daniel Roe, the last to give up, went to New Harmony to see how Owen's group was faring.

Downstream, the Owenites at New Harmony had set to work establishing an interim committee that assigned housing to men, women, and children and appointed them jobs. All children were to receive a free education and once everyone learned the "rational rules of cooperation" the community would blossom into a permanent society that would have no need of money or government. The group, however, failed to build an esprit de corps of idealists. Instead, wrangling broke out. Thomas Pears, an accountant who had convinced his wife to sell their possessions and relocate in New Harmony with their children, was given the job of keeping the community's books—the very occupation that he had grown weary of in Pittsburgh. Further exacerbating the situation, fever and chills—malaria—broke out as bottom land was opened up for farming. The resulting ague sapped people's strength and took the lives of those with weakened constitutions. Eventually, most of the able-bodied resorted to meeting at the tavern where people danced long into the night and where spirited debates occurred over how to run a perfect society.

As winter approached, the women began to voice their concerns about lack of clothing, food, and medical supplies. They also expressed doubts about the "free education" being offered to their children. Old Neef, the headmaster and a former lieutenant in Napoleon's army, carried a whistle around his neck and allotted his charges exactly fifteen minutes for each meal, demanding they must put their food in their mouths in unison. The committee recommended a dress code for the entire community—for men white pantaloons, buttoned over a boy's jacket, made of light material, without a collar; for women, a coat reaching to the knee and pantaloons. The costume was not universally adopted.[3]

By spring 1826 the community was embroiled in contentious bickering over a second and then a third constitution—finding it disheartening to come to grips with the realities of living under the arbitrary rule by committee. Factions set up two separate communities—Macluria and Feiba Peveli. When it was proposed that the main community be subdivided as well, the New Harmony *Gazette* suggested these new settlements be named Lovedale, Everblest, Glee, Lovely, Voltaire, Socrates, and Peace Glen. In the end, New Harmony was anything but harmonious. People deserted the place, despairing of ever establishing rules and guidelines under which everyone could cheerfully live in equanimity. They returned to their homes poorer but wiser, having learned that a utopian community will not come about overnight, that it takes more than a boatload of scholars and scientists, more than the good intentions of a wealthy philanthropist, to achieve heaven on earth. Such a venture requires a special depth of character in a society, a community of individuals who have the resilience to give and take in a learning environment characterized and sustained by mutual respect and the free interchange of ideas.

As Swedenborg understood, knowing is unique to each of us—a cookie-cutter education is not a true education. First-hand knowledge, especially when patterned with the wisdom of those who have gone before us, is a crucial way of knowing and, despite the pitfalls, may build for us a footbridge of understanding and wisdom that leads to higher ground. This is what the stories, poetry, and art of *Live & Learn* are all about. They help us understand this most enigmatic aspect of being human: what brings forth and taps the power of the questing spirit.

Notes

1. Buley, R. Carlyle. *The Old Northwest.* v. 2. Indianapolis, Indiana Historical Society, 1950. pp. 607–608.

2. Block, Marguerite. *The New Church in the New World: A Study of Swedenborgianism in America.* New York, Henry Holt & Co., 1932. p. 119.

3. Holloway, Mark. *Heavens on Earth: Utopian Communities in America 1680–1880.* 2d ed. New York, Dover Publications, 1966. pp. 111–112.

In Search of the Miraculous

I ONCE KNEW AN ARTIST who had spent some years immersed in the lore of the magical and the miraculous, especially those mysteries found in the Far East. He was convinced that the paranormal phenomena which had always eluded his search in the West would be easy to find in India. He managed to save enough money to go to India for one year, where he planned to study art and to seek out individuals who could demonstrate extraordinary powers.

In India, he visited a great many places, making lengthy and arduous journeys. Whenever he was told of a holy man or a guru or adept supposedly able to manifest *siddhis,* abilities thought to be miraculous or magical, he would trek there. In every case his efforts came to nothing. Sometimes at the end of a pilgrimage he would find only some wretched *fakir,* able to demonstrate nothing that was not commonplace in the streets of any large Indian city. Self-proclaimed wizards were obvious conjurers and charlatans preying upon the credulity of whatever followers they managed to gather.

Some who were supposed to be sorcerers told him that they could not demonstrate their powers for the merely curious. Since the artist could not persuade these sages of the seriousness of his interests, he had no way to evaluate their claims and so had to continue his search burdened by his ever-growing frustrations.

Finally, the time came for him to leave India. To his knowledge, not one siddha had he seen, nor one wizard had he encountered. Whether the supposed holy men or women were actually holy he couldn't say, and he certainly had not found the Teacher he had hoped to find to aid him in his own spiritual quest.

Ready to leave India, the artist walked down a street in Calcutta silently cursing all those who claimed to have powers beyond the ordinary. "All fakes," he muttered to himself. "Every last one of them fakes." He repeated this to himself over and over again. Suddenly, he raised his eyes and found himself gazing into the swarthy and unfriendly face of a man in a turban who stood across the street. For a moment the artist could hear his own words ringing in his ears. All at once, he felt as if he had been struck in the middle of his head with an axe. The pain was agonizing, and he fell to the street losing consciousness. Later he found himself being assisted to his feet by a passerby. The man in the turban was gone. The artist was left with what was absolutely the most terrible headache of his life. The unbearable pain persisted until he was about two days out to sea—when all at once it was gone.

The artist was excited to have what he felt was proof that what he had been seeking in the Far East really did exist. He decided that his search had been lacking in sufficient intensity or duration and resolved to return and renew his search.

He did eventually retrace his steps to India, and for a time lived in Nepal and in Tibet as well. Many wonders were revealed to him, and he achieved remarkable growth spiritually and as an artist.

And so, the artist who had doubted the authenticity of his initial experiences learned many valuable things—among them, that in order for learning to begin, like a book, the mind must first be opened. His act of returning to the place of his spiritual awakening exemplifies the heart of *Live & Learn.* For it is the realization at some deep, intuitive level that the will to learn and the will to teach are acts of love, that the quest for wisdom and its conveyance to others is nothing less than the manifestation of humanity's faith in the miraculous.

ROBERT MASTERS, co-founder and research director for The Foundation for Mind Research, is recognized as a leading pioneer in the consciousness-and-human potentials fields. Dr. Masters is author or co-author of twenty-five books and more than a hundred papers and articles related to his studies into human behavior and its potential. As the founder of the Association for the Masters Psychophysical Method, Dr. Masters has trained numerous teachers in psychophysical re-education.

Live & Learn

PERSPECTIVES ON THE QUESTING SPIRIT

PART I

The Spirit Adventurous

Florida

I'll tell you about Florida:
They've oranges and palms,
And tennis-courts and beaches,
And shells and pelicans.

And swamps with alligators,
And very splendid zoos,
And acrobatic dolphins,
Paellas and shrimp stews.

And weather up to boiling—
I appreciate all that.
But I came down from Albany,
And Florida is *flat!*

—Julia Randall

RAY SILVERMAN

I've Got It!

"WHEN THE SUN OF CONSCIOUSNESS FIRST SHONE UPON ME, behold a miracle!" wrote deaf–blind Helen Keller, ecstatically describing the moment when she first learned the significance of language and the reality of a world beyond her senses. Today the story of Helen's triumph over a triple handicap and the influence of her teacher, Anne Mansfield Sullivan, is familiar. It is especially well known among educators who marvel at Anne's ability to break through Helen's early resistance, melt her heart, and free her mind.

Less well known are the details of that story. Helen Keller was not an easy student. Recalling what it was like to be a six-year-old child, totally focused on satisfying her natural appetites, Helen later wrote:

> I was impelled like an animal to seek food and warmth . . . I was like an unconscious clod of earth. There was nothing in me except the instinct to eat, drink, and sleep. My days were a blank without past, present, or future, without hope or anticipation, without interest or joy.

Into that dark, silent world Anne Sullivan tried to bring the light of knowledge, a difficult task. Helen's parents, Captain and Mrs. Keller, pitied Helen, did not discipline her, and allowed her to become a terror in the home. When twenty-year-old Anne Sullivan came to live with the family as Helen's governess, she discovered that Helen was not only deaf, blind, and mute; it seemed that she was also untrainable, uneducable, and above all, incorrigible![1]

Anne described Helen as "an untamed little creature . . . a little savage" and said:

> The greatest problem I would have to solve is how to discipline and control her without breaking her spirit. I shall go rather slowly at first and try to win her love. I shall not try to conquer

Giorgio de Chirico.
The Seer.
Oil on canvas,
35½×27½ in., 1915.
The Museum of Modern Art, New York. James Thrall Soby Bequest. Photograph ©2001 The Museum of Modern Art, New York.

her by force alone; but I shall insist on reasonable obedience from the start.

Within two weeks, Anne had accomplished the first phase of Helen's educational program. Before Anne's eyes, Helen was transformed into a gentle child. The delighted teacher wrote:

> My heart is singing with joy this morning. A miracle has happened. The light of understanding has shone upon my little pupil's mind, and behold, all things are changed! The wild little creature has been transformed into a gentle child.

The next step was to learn the manual alphabet. Anne repeatedly touched and pressed Helen's hand with movements symbolizing the letters of the alphabet. Although there was some success as Helen learned to imitate the movements, there was no conscious connection in her mind between the letters being spelled into her hand and specific objects. "I had not the faintest idea what I was doing," wrote Helen. "I have only a tactile memory of my fingers going through those motions and changing from one position to another."

Helen and Anne went on like that for two more weeks with no further progress. Helen could not make the connection. By this time, Anne was discouraged, but she did not give up. Helen later wrote:

> In despair she led me out to the ivy-covered pump-house and made me hold the cup under the spout while she pumped. With the other hand she spelled *w-a-t-e-r* emphatically. I stood still, my whole body's attention fixed on the motions of her fingers as the cool stream flowed over my hand. All at once there was a strange stir within me—a misty consciousness, a sense of something remembered. It was as if I had come back to life after being dead!

Helen had learned that what Anne was doing with her fingers meant that the cold, wet liquid rushing over her hand had a word for itself. In that same moment, she realized that she could use these same hand signs to communicate with other people. Helen describes this experience as a breakthrough into a new level of consciousness.

> When the sun of consciousness first shone upon me, behold a miracle! The stock of my young life that had perished, now steeped in the waters of knowledge, grew again, budded again, was sweet with the blossoms of childhood. Down in the depths of my being I cried, "It is good to be alive." I held out two trembling hands to life, and in vain would silence impose dumbness upon me henceforth.
>
> That first revelation was worth all the years I had spent in dark, soundless imprisonment. That word 'water' dropped into my mind like the sun in a frozen winter world.

The story of Anne Sullivan and Helen Keller has always been an inspiration for educators. We wonder at the combination of firm discipline and gentle love that brings Helen to the point where she is ready to learn. We sympathize with Anne and admire her perseverance as she continues to seek a creative solution, even when she has reached the point of despair. And we rejoice with Helen as she discovers the meaning of language and the joy of communication. "I felt joyous, strong, equal to my limitations," writes Helen. *"Sweet, strange things that were locked up in my heart began to sing"* (emphasis added).

In his poem, "Sailing to Byzantium," William Butler Yeats writes:

An aged man is but a paltry thing,
A tattered coat upon a stick, unless
Soul clap its hands and sing, and louder sing.[2]

Sometimes in our teaching and learning, there are moments at the well—moments when the truth shines forth like sparkling water, and our soul claps its hands with joy. A teacher is inspired with a new way to get across a concept; a student cries out, "I've got it!" This miracle can occur at any time, in any place. We have sailed the seas and come to the holy city, to worship in the holy temple, to be baptized with water and spirit. And in this holy place, despite our limitations, and beyond every tatter in our mortal dress, our souls begin to sing, and louder sing . . .

RAY SILVERMAN received a doctorate in English and education from the University of Michigan, a master of arts in teaching from Wesleyan University, and a master of divinity from the Academy of the New Church Theological School, Bryn Athyn, Pennsylvania. He has served as pastor to congregations in Pittsburgh and Atlanta and is currently Assistant Professor of Religion at Bryn Athyn College of the New Church. He is editor and revisor of Helen Keller's spiritual autobiography, *Light in My Darkness* (Chrysalis Books: 1994, 2000), and is the co-author, with his wife, Star, of *Rise Above It: Spiritual Development through the Ten Commandments* (Touchstone Seminars: 2000).

Notes
1. Helen Keller was born on June 27, 1880. At nineteen months of age she contracted an illness which left her deaf, blind, and unable to speak. On March 3, 1887, Anne Sullivan came to her home to be her governess. In her later years Helen referred to the date of Anne's arrival as her "soul's birthday."
2. "Byzantium" in Yeats' poetry is a symbol of heaven, a country of eternal youth and abundant vitality. The poem begins with the words, "That is no country for old men." Emanuel Swedenborg writes: "In heaven all are in the flower of their youth and remain in it to eternity" (Paragraph 250:2, *Marriage Love*).

RUTH LATTA

Meeting Virginia Woolf at the Station

Oscar Bluemner. *Flag Station, Elizabeth, New Jersey*. Watercolor on paper, 12½×9¼ in. The Metropolitan Museum of Art. Bequest of Charles F. Ikle, 1963. 64.27.9.

WHY DON'T YOU JUST TRY TO BE FUNNY? This thought occurs to Sally on their friends' doorstep. After two weeks in England, she and Rick are now back home in Ottawa, hoping to tell about their trip without provoking yawns.

"I failed in a literary pilgrimage," she begins. People like stories of plans gone awry. Their host leans forward, smiling in anticipation.

"The last day, we drove south from London through Kent and Sussex. We had to return the car to the rental office by six PM, then check into the airport hotel. I think by the end of our holiday Rick was getting tired of my writers' shrines, but there was one famous author's house that I had to see. We were driving down a major highway and we saw the name of the village, Rodmell, but there was no turnoff."

The hills swept back from the road, down through the valley of the Ouse. One hill shaped like a hog's back, was deep purple. Through the open window I could smell the sea. Then I spied the name of the village.

"There's the turn!" Rick was driving so fast that before I got the words out we were past it. We had to go several miles further to find a place to turn around.

"So he drove back, getting that look on his face . . ."

"We had to be back by six . . ." Rick interjects.

"I know. We found the road I'd spotted, a gravel road, very narrow. We went along it for a bit, watching it wind upward and disappear in a wood, and then we came to a little railway station—the one on the map in the front of her published diaries—but it was barricaded on both sides by a wire mesh fence and padlocked. The building looked long out of use. . . ."

SALLY PULLED OUT THE AUTHOR'S PUBLISHED DIARY and showed Rick the railway station in the simple map in the frontispiece. "I know that's the road."

"The car can't climb the fence."

They stared at each other. She knew he was waiting for her to say, "Let's forget it." She said nothing because her heart was racing. She was so close.

A small truck approached the station from the opposite side. A man in denim overalls and rubber boots got out, unlocked the fences and brought the vehicle through. Sally held her breath.

The man pulled up beside their car and thrust his red face through the open window. "You can't go through that way!" he bellowed. "Where were you thinking of going?"

"To Rodmell. I guess you have to go through Lewes first, right?"

The farmer nodded. "Tourists! I'll let you through this once, but don't make a practice of it."

They passed through, over the tracks and along a road which wound upward, with trees on either side.

"It can't have changed much from when she used to ride her bicycle here or walk here with her dog," Sally told Rick. "She and her husband went for walks all the time here." Rick did not reply. . . .

"ANYWAY," SALLY CONTINUES, "a farmer let us through, and we got to the village, but we couldn't see any sign directing us to the house. Odd, as it belongs to the National Trust. We went through the village and out the other side, and then Rick stopped at a gas station and asked. We were directed down this sloping, narrow side street. The view across the fields was beautiful."

"A cul de sac," interrupts Rick "Big, new houses crowded on a one-lane street with a school at the bottom of the hill. The children were just getting out. The kids were like ants all over the place."

"Then I spied the house," says Sally. "The plaque on the door read: 'Closed Fridays.'"

The hostess groans. "So you never got in?"

"No. I asked Rick to park so we could walk back and see the grounds or peek in. He said, 'I can't park. I may not be able to get the car out of here. If you want a picture, snap it from the window.'"

The host and hostess chuckle.

"With a rented car, driving on a crowded lane, and on the wrong side of the road, I don't blame Rick for being annoyed. Did you get a picture?"

"A blurry one."

"Poor Sally! Will this harm your writing?" The hostess is sarcastic. "You missed the chance to pick up positive vibrations from your role model."

"She's not exactly a role model. I'll have to be content reading her diaries."

The hostess, laughing, goes to make coffee.

Sally's hostess always expresses amazement at Rick's toleration of Sally's writing. In the era of the two-career couple, with women entering the labor force in record numbers, Sally, at home with her computer, is clearly out of step. The hostess is retired from a long and prosperous civil service career. The arts, to her, mean season tickets to the English drama series at the National Arts Centre or an annual trip to Stratford. The actual creation of literature is for bohemians or neurasthenic members of the British upper-middle classes, certainly not for Sally, who takes her little hobby too seriously.

As Rick and the host talk about the cutbacks in the civil service, Sally leans back, thinking of the failed trip to Rodmell. . . .

AFTER THAT SPECIAL DISPENSATION TO CROSS THE RAILROAD TRACKS, how disappointing! Not wanting Rick to see her tears, she stared out at the landscape as they drove toward Lewes and the major highway. The sun gleamed on the hills.

"Can you check the map and tell me which motorway connects Lewes to Gatwick?" Rick demanded.

Sally turned to the map and identified a highway.

A fight would have ended the vacation on a sour note. Overseas vacations were a rarity to Sally, and she did not want to quarrel. She couldn't expect Rick to feel the strange excitement that came over her at the thought: *She knew this landscape.* Rick was generous, competent, and understanding. Many husbands were much less.

The trip, after ten years of marriage, was a celebration. Ten years earlier, others said the marriage wouldn't last. She had tied the knot while still shaken over the death of her first husband. As for Rick, he was trying to cast off the trauma of an unhappy live-in relationship.

Sally trembles, remembering her first month in Rick's apartment. She knew no one in the city but Rick. He left daily for work, taking the elevator down to the parking garage. Looking down, she saw his car as a toy vehicle in a cloud of exhaust fumes.

Some days the snow-covered landscape merged with breath and fog, and everything over the edge of the balcony was totally white. Sometimes she panicked. She had ceased to exist! Exploring the city was possible on good days, but often the weather was bad, and she felt marooned on a cold planet, dependent on Rick's telephone calls and homecomings, which seemed a miracle each evening at six.

The awareness that her feelings were childish, even crazy, and inappropriate for a would-be independent woman, did not help. Then she discovered the library nearby. Reading *Mrs. Dalloway* and *To the Lighthouse*, seeing how the writer experimented with time, gave her courage. In the characters' minds, thoughts and fears impinged pell-mell, past memories blurred with future hopes.

The novels got her through the winter. In time her rational self was reborn and found work to do, places to go, people to see.

ON THEIR WAY HOME THAT EVENING, Rick turns to Sally. "I wasn't trying to be mean, that day at Rodmell. I was afraid we wouldn't get the car back by six."

"I wish I hadn't told that story. I was only trying to be amusing."

"We'll go back to Rodmell next time."

"Sure." Someday.

That night, Sally can't sleep. She goes down to the living room, in order not to disturb Rick. The furnishings of their daily life together are reassuring. She takes down a paperback volume of the writer's diary. It is reassuring, too. Written years before Sally was born, the author's thoughts are like a letter from an intelligent and honest friend. However often she reads them the diaries always contain something new. Now, she comes upon an entry which has never registered before—an anecdote about a trip to the station.

The writer stood outside her cottage and listened to the sound of a train in the distance, the last train that night. Her husband was coming home from London. Although it was a windy, wet night, she set out by bicycle to meet him.

Was there any logical reason to suppose he would not appear? Another woman? No, just the ever-present fear of losing the one person essential to one's existence.

Crossing fields in the wind and rain, barely able to see in the moonless night with only a flashlight, she stopped her bicycle under a tree, overwhelmed with anxiety. Intense loneliness seized her. She stood frozen.

Finally she rallied. "If he's not at the station, I'll simply go up to London myself," she told herself. She got onto her bicycle and continued, though she often dropped her flashlight and had to get off and walk.

The station was illuminated. Smiling happy couples moved about hand in hand, making her feel more alone than ever. She bought a ticket to London and went inside to wait. Then, around a corner, came her husband, looking chilly and cross.

To cover her ecstatic, wild feeling of having been saved—from what?—she greeted him, then fiddled with her bicycle, pretending to fix it. She then slipped off to the ticket office for a refund.

On the way home he told her his troubles, oblivious to the crisis she had been through and her great relief at being with him again.

Though the station was unnamed, Sally knows it's the one she and Rick had passed. Fifty years later, it is no longer used for passenger traffic, barricaded on either side by wire mesh. The woman's terrified journey there, her calmer trip home, had been along that steep road under the large leafy trees.

Sally knows just how Virginia Woolf felt. She has read much about her. Some biographers said her husband, Leonard, was a saint, giving her everything, receiving little in return. Others said he was domineering. Before Woolf drowned herself, she left Leonard a note: "I don't think any two people could be as happy as we have been." Some saw it as a testament to her love. Others say she wanted to spare him guilt.

Back upstairs, Sally watches Rick breathe. She feels close to him. Should she wake him? Although she knows of no objective standard of measuring happiness, she suspects that, in important ways, she and Rick are happier than the famous writer and her husband. There are advantages to being ordinary. Sally is no tortured genius. She will never collect stones in her pockets to drown herself in Mooney's Bay.

She sets Virginia's diary on the bedside table. In the dark she visualizes the author's deep-set eyes.

"I've learned from your work," she whispers. "Someday I'll visit your house."

RUTH LATTA's latest book, *Grace MacInnis: A Woman to Remember,* is published by Xlibris. She lives in Ottawa, Canada.

RALPH E. PRAY

"Let Me Show You How It Works"

MY FIRST DAY ON A COLLEGE CAMPUS begins after I catch the south-bound bus out of Santa Fe. For the trip I wear the beige gabardine western suit bought in El Paso on army mustering-out day. Beneath the long, square-cut jacket is the elegant, gold-embroidered vest Tedi made and a pastel necktie she knitted to go with the ensemble.

It's a momentous day for me, a Korean War Vet off to my first college day at age twenty-six. Out of uniform a short time before, my steps are long. I have no debts. My arms are ready to hug the

Irene Rice Pereira.
Man and Machine.
Oil on canvas,
47½×34¾ in., 1936.
The University of Arizona
Museum of Art.
Gift of Edward
J. Gallagher Jr. 62.5.4.

world, to thank everyone for letting me come back from the Far East. No one could sing a more happy song.

I'm headed for the New Mexico Institute of Mining and Technology at Socorro, sixty-five miles south of Albuquerque. The highway south of Santa Fe is an old friend, hitchhiked across every weekend out of Guided Missile School in Texas before going overseas. I close my eyes and smile at the memory of the eager trips, ten months of them, north across blistering desert and freezing cold to Tedi and *The City Different*.

THE BUS STATION IN SOCORRO is near a corner of the old plaza. My suitcase marks me as an obvious newcomer. I catch a ride with a friendly student to the campus a mile out of town.

"Just starting?" he asks.

"Yeah. I'm signing up for metallurgy. What do you take?"

"Geology. But met's good too. They have a big lab. Where do you want to be dropped?"

"I'd sure like to see the lab."

"Fine," he says. "I'm in married housing, near the Met Lab. I'll deliver you. It's only a short walk from there to the Ad Building."

He drives onto the east end of the quiet campus and swings into an empty parking lot beside an old red-brick building. "There it is," he points. "Doubt if anyone's around today."

"Thanks a lot, anyway."

He pulls away as I set my heavy suitcase on the front sidewalk. The stained stone letters above the double doors read *Metallurgy Building*. I climb the wide staircase and open one of the doors. A stairway goes up. I follow it to see a high-ceilinged room with small furnaces and rows of tables. Not much. I go downstairs past the main landing into the basement. There, spread out in a large room, are all kinds of machines. I recognize a familiar shape, a rock crusher, so small I wonder if it's useful. But there's an electric motor with it, and a belt drive. Now I see other familiar shapes. There are ball mills, crushing rolls, mineral jigs, a concentrating table, each with its own electric motor. But so small the machines remind me of the Christmas morning I got my first large mechanical toys. I'm walking around between the things, exclaiming over and over, "I'll be damned."

My Wilfley concentrating table unit at Santa Fe County's Tom Payne Mine before Korea was seventeen feet long in its entirety and weighed over a thousand pounds. Here is the same unit, ready to turn on, but so small I can pick it up and carry it under one arm. I search for words—toyland!

I feel a strong attachment to the little machines. Their presence and the familiar smell of process chemicals makes me feel I've been here before, even though this is the first time I've ever been on a college campus. My senses embrace this place, reminding me of my teenage months at the remote lead mine in Nevada, then drilling silver ore at the Sunshine Mine in Idaho, and working thousands of feet below the surface at the Star shaft in Burke the next summer. I think of my widow-maker's job in the U.S. Mine in Bingham, Utah, and the process mill machinery in all those western mining camps.

There had never been time for me to go to college. The challenge of going down a thousand-foot mine shaft at fifty feet per second, or loading and shooting a half-case of dynamite in my deep underground drill holes, simply pushed the thought of college attendance right off the map. My education as a young working man had been broad, rich in its contact with hard-hat people, sometimes violent, always fascinating. I wondered if I was addicted to risk, why the adrenaline rush pushed me into sparsely-populated regions. Then came Korea and the draft and a year of army school. High tech. I had seen the light.

The big risk is in not getting educated to a level where I can lend an effective hand to everyone. I need a formal education. I hope this is a stopping point, a place for me to stay and learn about deep reasoning, the beginning of a new life.

Around me there are strange-looking contraptions with legs, arms, bowls, and belts. I read the nameplates. I know what most of them do from having read books about mineral processing. I study the machines one by one.

"Hello," a man's voice calls from the stairway area.

"Hi." I walk over to a comfortable-looking man, about forty-five, wearing white buckskin shoes and a rumpled suit. He has a kind grin, a dark mustache.

"I'm Lefty Thompson."

"I'm Ralph Pray." We shake hands.

"Is that your suitcase out on the sidewalk?"

"Yes sir. I just got here from Santa Fe and wanted to see the Met Lab. I couldn't wait. I'm a freshman in metallurgy."

"Well, by golly. Welcome. I'm the head of the met department."

"Thank you, sir." He's still smiling at me. I feel very comfortable with him. "Do all these little things work?"

"They sure do. This is where research and development, R and D, actually begins. What would you like to see?" He reaches his hand out to invite me. "Go ahead and turn something on."

"I'd sure like to see the Wilfley table crank up."

"It's all yours."

We walk to the far wall where the Wilfley sits on a sturdy bench. I turn the motor on. The table operates with a familiar thump. It's used to separate heavy solids from light solids in water after fine-grinding the ore. It takes gold out of sand right before your eyes.

"Ever see a big concentrator run?" he asks.

"Yes sir. I re-decked the Wilfley at the Tom Payne up in Santa Fe County, and operated all winter. We shipped thirteen tons of table concentrate to the El Paso smelter. That was before Korea."

"I've heard about that mill from Horace Moses. He's New Mexico's senior mining engineer. So you were at the Tom Payne when it ran a few years ago?"

"Yes sir. I lived and worked there as a partner. Mr. Moses visited us. He's one of my sponsors here at the school. What is that strange-looking rig over there?" I ask, pointing to an unfamiliar unit.

"That's an electrostatic separator. Let me show you how it works." He takes an hour or so to explain the machines I don't know much about. We're standing at the stairway looking back into the room before leaving. "What do you think of all this?" he asks.

"It took us six months to build the mill at the Tom Payne before we knew the process would work. It seems like I could have brought a sample from the mine into this room and found the same answer in one day."

"That's what R and D is. You just hit the nail on the head."

I'm beside myself with excitement because rich ore can be found to feed these babies. I have visions of a small truck backing up to these nifty toys, of testing my gold ore samples from the Ortiz Mountains.

"Can I bring some ore in here and do test work?" I ask.

"That's the best possible use," he says. "Nothing would please me more. I'll help you in any way I can."

I feel a strong kinship. "Thank you, sir. A friend up north gave me a sample of copper ore from his mine to assay. Can I find out how that's done?"

"I'll show you right here tomorrow, after you settle in. We'll do the assay on your sample together and then you'll do it by yourself before supper time. How's that?"

"Wow!" I think he has a heart of gold. After thanking Lefty a couple times I lug my suitcase over to administration. The dormitory person gives me a key to a single room in Driscoll Hall. I move in. My window looks out over the entire green campus, clear to the end where I can see the front of the Met Lab, the place where my past and my future just met with a strong, new hope. The day ends with exultation. My life is changing.

Midyear registration in the small college begins and ends the next morning. Orientation takes thirty minutes for each department. The speeches are given by professors with help from graduate students in petroleum, geophysics, geology, and mining. Most of the new fellows are interested in geology. The metallurgy section orientation takes place last, just before lunch. We're all in Levis standing around in front of the met lab waiting for Professor Thompson, whose office is in another building.

He walks over to us. "Good morning, freshmen. Welcome to the Metallurgy Department. I'm Lefty Thompson. We're going to break this orientation into two parts. Dr. Greene will take you through the analytical part of it upstairs, where he teaches fire assay classes. But first we'll leave the usual procedure by moving into the process department where a new student will conduct the metallurgy orientation."

He looks at me with a smile. "Ralph, this class is yours for the next hour."

RALPH E. PRAY holds degrees from the University of Alaska and the Colorado School of Mines and has traveled widely in his work in mineral property evaluation. Dr. Pray owns an independent research laboratory in Los Angeles County, has taught engineering at the university level, and has been writing for publication for forty-five years.

ALAN PUCCIARELLO

Child Therapy

For three years I have worked with you
while you have done nothing
but love me, your small being
reaching through its odd mind to ask
if you can be me when you're older, when I die.
Now I understand that the tyrannosaurus in your hand
every week, biting, bitter and
storming away from his dinosaur friends.
You tell your mother, your teachers, anyone who will listen,
that you cannot wait for this one day's one hour
        to play our games
and then you must leave.

I am a large beast
once left for extinct with my small brain,
old fear and sheer hunger
and yet you keep coming
so much closer though you are younger than I
to teach, to feed me, blood, life
your heart torn and raw with attachment.

ALAN PUCCIARELLO is a poet and child psychotherapist living, practicing, and writing in Vermont. His work has appeared in the *Hampden-Sydney Poetry Review* and *Beauty for Ashes*.

HEATHER HEILMAN

The Student You Can't Set on Fire

COUNTING PRESCHOOL AND KINDERGARTEN, I've spent twenty-four years of my life as a student. By the time I picked up my master's hood at the age of thirty, I was thoroughly unenamored with school and assumed with relief I'd come to the end of my formal education. Back in grade school, in the preamble to a standardized test, there was a question asking what level of education I planned on completing. How was a fifth-grader supposed to know? But I took my number two pencil and filled in the oval next to "master's degree." Even then, a Ph.D. seemed like just too much. But now my master's degree doesn't seem like enough. It hasn't cured my suspicions that my education has been deeply inadequate. I'm thinking of going back to school.

My mother says I hated school from the very beginning. There were tears, fights, sulks, and occasional requests to be home schooled. Like nearly everyone, I was sometimes bored or frustrated in the classroom, but the real problem wasn't aversion to education but the social environment that went with it. And even this wasn't universally bad. At my suburban Catholic grade school, I found friends who indulged my imagination and allowed me to direct them in games of Witchy-Poo versus the Fairies. In fourth-grade I had a warm proto-flirtation with the dorkily bespectacled but potentially hunksome Carlos Havia. But at the same time, I was dreaming of growing up to be the bionic woman or the smart *Charlie's Angel,* and what I most wanted to do with my future super-powers was to get revenge. I wanted revenge on Sister Beatrice, because I was too scared

Fernand Léger.
Woman with a Book.
Oil on canvas,
45¾×32⅛ in.,1923.
The Museum of Modern
Art, New York. Nelson A.
Rockefeller Bequest.
Photograph ©2001
The Museum of Modern
Art, New York.

to ask her permission to go to the bathroom and peed on the floor. I wanted revenge on Germaine of the beautiful, long, blonde curls, who always got to play the Blessed Virgin in Christmas pageants and May crownings. I wanted revenge on my best friend's older sister, who called me a space cadet.

I was a budding freak or, in kinder terms, an eccentric. A junior space cadet could find a little space for herself in grade school but in junior high things were harder. I was too serious, too quiet, I owned no Jordache jeans, my Nikes were seasons out of date, even my shoe laces were wrong. My former best friend dropped me, and I turned viciously on my only remaining friend because she was an even bigger dork than I was, and I despised her for it.

Although there are undoubtedly bits of information still lodged in my brain that were learned in my junior high school classes—maybe the bare basics of cell biology, the relationship of Celsius to Fahrenheit, or the rudiments of why economic inflation happens—I remember almost nothing of my classes from those years. The only teacher, who made an impression was my sixth-grade teacher, Mr. Biddle, who looked like a Sonny Bono impersonator, assigned us magazine reports instead of book reports, and lent me (his star student) an incomprehensible New-Age book called *Pyramid Power.*

In high school the fog of misery began to thin out a bit. Still, those are years I would not be happy to repeat, however much I long for a second chance. And then there was the pointless muddle of my freshman year of college. I crowned the end of that year by flunking a Spanish class in which I'd been averaging a B because I was confused about the time of the final, and too dispirited to ask the professor for a make-up. Instead I dropped out.

What was the point of school when there was life to be lived? I would educate myself. I would Read. I would Live. I didn't need a bachelor's degree to write a novel. I had a big, fat spiral notebook, and I began to write what would have been an execrable novel.

I suspected my work sucked, and never let anyone read it. I was worried. I was more than worried; I was in the midst of a vocational crisis that would last for the better part of a decade. What if I was no good at writing? What if writing for a living or part of a living or even just modest publication was something beyond my capabilities?

My temporary solution was to declare that it didn't matter anyway because no one read anymore and literature was dead. Why would someone with grandiose ambitions want to waste her time in a venture as moribund as the writing of books? I was full of myself. I wanted to shake up the world. Therefore, I wanted to be a filmmaker.

This might have been the dumbest idea I ever pursued, though the competition is fierce. But it had one redeeming feature. No one could reasonably expect me to learn film production on my own, so I could go back to school.

I went to Memphis State University, a questionable choice for someone who wanted to be a visionary director. It was a campus of ugly, squarish red-brick buildings. I made no friends there during my undergraduate years. I was lonely, dispirited, and unmoored. But there were times after class, walking across that unlovely campus, when I would be infused with an unexpected joy. There is something inherently right and good about learning. To learn is to be transformed and allowed to hope.

At first, the best classes were the film history courses that involved watching and writing about old movies. I was introduced to Howard Hawks and Preston Sturges, as well as Fellini and Antonioni. These classes seemed too entertaining to be scholarly legitimate. Watching a film, even one directed by Ingmar Bergman, does not demand as much as reading Tolstoy. Still, I learned something about how to think about a work of art.

As I grew disenchanted with my chosen medium, classes in literature and history became my reason for getting up in the morning. Math and sciences were either dull or incomprehensible or both, often taught by burned out academicians with little passion for teaching, or their assistants who had more enthusiasm but even fewer communication skills than their seniors. I'm sad that the hard sciences were too much for me. A whole system for understanding the world seems to be closed to me.

When people decide to change their lives, they go back to school. We expect education to give us power, wisdom, economic security, prestige, and peace of mind. But our educations cost us something too, besides tuition dollars. We should keep learning all our lives, we are told. We will retain a certain youth if we constantly shake up our brains with new knowledge and new skills to learn. But there can be a negative side to prolonging our formal education. If we spend too much time in school too early, we can excessively prolong our apprenticeship to life and avoid growing up.

I finished my bachelor's degree one December and started work on my master's in January. I went to graduate school because I wanted to keep learning about writing, but also because I couldn't think of what else to do. I worried that professional studenthood might not be the best thing I could be doing with my time. Other people my age had salaries and new cars, even mortgages and babies. I had finals and term papers. All that separated my classmates and me from undergraduates was a few years, an extra degree, and a growing mood of desperation. I was miserable and so were most of my classmates. We couldn't seem to figure out what to do next. We still didn't know what we wanted to do when we grew up, or we knew but we didn't know how to do it. Our choices seemed no more appealing than those of a high-school dropout. We envied our old friends their salaries, but not their jobs. We liked the freedom of being students and slackers, but not the poverty. We knew what the academic job market was like, and we couldn't realistically plan on being professors. Anyway, we knew from long exposure to our teachers that their work could be as pointless and soul-crushing as any other.

A workable future came when I published an article in a local magazine, which led to further assignments. I left the university to pursue my MFA through a nontraditional low-residency program, one with many students far more accomplished than I and one that didn't allow me to live on an assistantship and student loans. I began to make part of my living as a writer and the rest at whatever part-time or temporary job worked for the moment. For the first time I felt I had a real life, albeit one far less glamorous than I had wished for.

It's been more than a year since I finished my degree, the longest period I've spent out of school in a decade. I miss it. I miss the rhythms and seasons of the academic year. Autumn has lost its sense of promise and is now only the harbinger of the coming cold. I want to go back. I want to keep learning. I want another chance to become wise. But there are other things I want. I want to work and make money and write a book and travel and volunteer. I want to read for pleasure and think my own thoughts. I want to pay off my student loans.

Since finishing this essay, HEATHER HEILMAN has accepted a job at Tulane University in New Orleans. Free graduate-school tuition is one of the fringe benefits.

RICHARD C. COLLINS

Playing with Heart

Carl Milles.
Fountain of the Muses.
Brookgreen Gardens,
Murrells Inlet, South
Carolina.

I DON'T SUPPOSE ANYONE is really thinking that after reading this article about teaching oneself to play the piano, he or she will sit at the piano and be able to play a favorite song. Hardly.

But readers will understand, if I have done my job, how it is that our piano students are so scared of performing, and why most teachers haven't been able to do much about it. But, to be fair, I'll continue on, so I can tell everyone how piano teaching can be drastically improved, and why all it takes to do so is a change of attitude.

I'll start with a typical student recital. We've all seen it before. A rather thin young lady enters from the wings, slithers across the stage, appearing not at all to notice that the audience is there, much less acknowledge their applause with a bow, and quickly seats herself at the piano. With a kind of hopeless shrug, she throws herself into her performance. And what comes out? Sometimes broken patches, the excellent mixing at will with the incoherent. Perhaps a flat, even-paced, rather dull, but accurate performance. Worse yet, an entrance into the piece, which rather quickly crumbles, to be replaced by another entrance, which again crumbles, and again an entrance, and again, until in tears she rushes off, determined, with some justice, never to do that again.

Of course, our young friend complains. "If only I hadn't been so nervous! I really knew the piece much better than that."

This nervousness is really a symptom of a more general condition. Young performers today lack conscious control over their playing. Nervous or not, when something goes wrong, when they make a mistake or have a memory slip, their unconscious habits are broken and they become stuck and can't go on. All their many hours of practicing do not help them a bit. Their only recourse is to start over.

But let's think about the performance situation a minute. In addition to creating nervousness, it can also produce moments of divine inspiration, where everything goes right and is seemingly effortless, the music flowing by on its own, without our being concerned about the details of how we do this or that. We call this "divine inspiration." And that's exactly what it is. Naturally, everyone seeks this magical state.

So why do we more often than not get something else? Why do performances crumble so easily? The problem is, I think, that piano study has traditionally been the narrow pursuit of a goal: the perfect performance. The student practiced every passage, every trill, every note, until the piece was mastered technically. But even this meticulous study was unable to produce consistently meaningful performances. The student was unable to break away from the mechanical habits induced by this kind of practice.

But, not to despair, some teachers found that there is another way, a way of being more receptive, which can lead to piano mastery. By *receptive* is meant being open at every moment of performance, and in every moment of practicing, to the inner guidance which is available to every person. Some call this guidance divine, and indeed it probably is, but it is located within us, and need not be sought outside.

Reliance on this aspect of ourselves does not eliminate the need for practice nor the need for discipline. Far from it. It merely opens the doors within us to a part of ourselves which is always ready and available. And when drawn upon it can make our practicing into a performance, our work into pleasure, and our every effort becomes imbued with creativity instead of drudgery.

So what happens in the "inspired" performance?

I think the first thing to realize is that we are not really conscious of all the thousands of impulses that go into producing a beautiful, uplifting performance. In our best work we are mainly conscious of the *effect* we are striving for at any given moment, but the particular *means* to achieve this effect we most often leave to our unconscious.

I mean that just how far to move the wrist, the position the fingers are in, just exactly the speed of a melodic ornament, the degree of tempo fluctuation here or there, all these are left to our unconscious to control. Our conscious mind, in contrast, is more concerned with the whole, and with how the character and energy of each section as we are creating it will work in that whole and produce that whole.

When we are truly inspired we let the physical and musical details happen as they will. Yet they happen with a kind of logic, certainty, and vitality unattainable with the closest analysis or with the utmost mental effort.

Is this a mystery? I don't think so. What is happening in these supreme moments is that a higher source takes over the actual running of the ship, as it were, and we are left free to plot the course and enjoy the ride. Very often this higher source also feeds us the plan, as well as the execution. A neat trick, of course, but what do we have to do in our practicing to make it possible to achieve this pinnacle of performance? What method can we use if all must be somehow so flexible in performance that it can obey the precise but changeable directions given by the inspiration of the moment? In short, how do we practice for an improvisation?

The solution, it seems to me, is to emphasize the improvisatory nature of the music from the beginning so that *whenever* we experience the piece, whether it is the earliest period of our study or during a performance, the conscious mind will always be concerned with conceptions of character and shape, and the fingers and arms will always be willingly, and usually unconsciously, working to manifest these conceptions.

It means learning your music "by ear" so that the sound you produce on the piano always starts with a sound-image in your mind, and it is that sound-image which directs the fingers. The pathway established will start from the imagination, then through the hearing part of the mind, to the fingers, and then to the actual sound produced, not the more usual pathway of one finger-movement connected to the next, and to the next, etc.

But how does the teacher go about teaching this more flexible "conscious" way of playing the piano?

First, let me say that the whole point of piano lessons, in my belief, is that the teacher must train the student to teach himself, not just to be a "good boy," and do everything the teacher says. Instead, the teacher needs to enable the student to draw upon the higher centers of the mind in a consistent and successful way. He must train the student to expand his musical imagination.

The teacher, for instance, can help the student to become mentally stimulated by asking him questions. This gets the student to form connective links in his mind. If the teacher puts the links there himself, it is not the same. He needs to find musical situations that in themselves pose a question. This way the student is compelled to seek the answer himself. Then when he finds the answer it is his, not the teacher's.

How this works is that the teacher can ask the younger student, "How should this sound?" or "What is the character of this section?" Of course, many young students will not yet have acquired the vocabulary to convert their feelings into words. Or, they may need a stimulus from the teacher before they could even conceive that all these various notes could produce a single concept, and so the teacher must then supply one of those colorful *miracle* words, such as *crystalline* or *somber* to get them started. When the student appears completely tongue-tied, I have found it useful to ask him if it should be say, *brassy,* or *grandiose,* or *fierce,* just to give him the chance to decide for himself. Thus he becomes more responsible for figuring out how to produce the particular character that he has decided upon, rather than just following the teacher's suggestions as to what to do.

Of course, training the mind to form a concept that concerns itself with the *whole thing* is partner to being able to use the mind to form a *sound-image* before asking the fingers to play. Both are really part of the same package. The imagination creates a whole sound-concept, and the body takes it from there.

So much for how to teach conscious involvement in the musical performance. Now we get to the thing which holds us back every time, and this is "perfectionitis." What is a perfect performance, anyway? I suppose one could say that something was "perfect" if it could not be improved upon. I don't think I have to belabor the fallaciousness of that idea in any of the arts. We all know that a work or a performance might be different from another, and we may even speak of one being "better" than another, but isn't that mostly a matter of taste, rather than a set of standards that we hold up and by which we judge what we are confronting?

The best thing to say to students is, "Perfection is an ideal and can be approached but never realized." When young performers get that idea firmly in their minds, nervousness, of necessity, will begin to disappear.

The importance of not trying to "*do* a perfect one," but instead "*make* a good one" cannot be brought out too strongly. After all, mistakes do happen. When they are forgotten as soon as they occur, the remainder of a performance can still be intact, but when the first little mistake becomes a disaster of major importance and destroys the composure of the performer because it breaks the imagined bubble of the perfect rendition, then the effect of the music as a whole suffers. It is almost as if when you plan from the point of view of an improviser you are beyond mistakes. The moment is all that counts. And when that moment is filled with love of the music, rather than worry about what might go wrong, at least you will have a fighting chance of making something worthwhile.

What can we learn from all this? And what does this discussion have to do with talent and gift?

Talent is free, but gift must be earned. And how do we receive this divine gift? We cannot ask for it, but instead, must earn it with our love of the music. We empty ourselves of our ego, our selfish point of view, and through dedication to the beauty left to us by generations of composers, we learn discipline and even self-realization. When we are thus opened up, the higher forces can find in us a proper vehicle through which to present to the world the uplifting benefits of great music.

As Herman Hesse says in *Siddharta*, "When someone is seeking, it happens quite easily that he only sees the thing he is seeking; that he is unable to find anything, unable to absorb anything, because he is thinking only of the thing he is seeking, because he has a goal, because he is obsessed with his goal. Seeking means: to have a goal, but finding means: to be receptive, to have no goal."

Or, to put it more simply: when you reach the point that you can stop asking questions, then you will begin to get the answers.

RICHARD SIDNEY COLLINS (1928–2001). a pianist and composer trained classically, received bachelor's and master's degrees from the Juilliard Institute. He studied with Pietro Scarpini in Italy on a Fulbright grant, and later earned a doctorate in performance from the University of Michigan. Dr. Collins performed as a jazz musician in his New York years.

LYNN VALENTE

The Writing Teacher

She sits in a large
flowered chair, our queen
of impossibility.

She brings out the box
of matches she has gathered
all week for us. We

bring our paper, hold it
to her light. The air
crackles with depression,

the cat's fur begins to rise.
What else have we
brought? We ourselves
are last to know.
We lean forward
to see—all our huge fires
hoping to be bright.

LYNN VALENTE teaches high-school Spanish in Vermont. She has studied with Sharon Olds in Rhode Island and participates regularly in writing workshops led by Kate Gleason and Jan Frazier—the subject of this poem. Lynn's poetry has appeared in a variety of small-press publications.

Victorian Home Schooling

Frank Sewall Educates His Daughters

Alice Archer Sewall James [1870–1955], artist, poet, play-wright, and teacher, prepared memoirs of her education as part of her application for a Guggenheim fellowship in 1946. Her recollections have been edited and abridged by Alice B. Skinner.

AROUND THE PARLOR, with its bare waxed and inlaid floor, my little sisters and I sat awaiting the prelude to the dance to come to the pause, when my father, looking up from his flying hands on the key-board, would announce "Signorina Madelina" or "Signorina Alicia," or whoever out of the four was to be the performer of the *pas seul*. Then out the child would fly to the center, in front of the coal grate, with the *Sistine Madonna* above it blessing the evening play, and my mother, with the baby on her lap, clapping for the encore. The dances were to be expressive of the music, and no one could tell what that might be, as the improvisation poured out every mood, changing its beat and character from *largo* to *vivace* with dramatic suddenness. Maud, with her heavy golden curls, was noted among us for the ra-pidity of her tiptoes. The breathless joy ended all too soon in the good-night kisses before going up to bed.

Morning prayers were always in the library around the tiled and mottoed chimney piece, with the busts of Swedenborg, Raphael, and

Socrates presiding over the tall bookcases, and the four Evangelists in the stained-glass tops of the high windows. The porch door of the library was open, in summer, to the shadow of the great willow tree, where serious talks with my father were held when faculty or visiting trustees sat in long conferences with long cigars. The College [Urbana University]—was a constant presence, an enveloping breath of distinction quite apart from person or place or even numbers or size. Consciously we sensed adventure from the Divine.

Spiritual adventure was kept alive in other ways, too. I remember taking from the bound music volumes near me on the piano seat a rather heavy book and, after opening it and playing a short movement, leaving it quickly to go with imperative announcement to interrupt my father writing under the Evangelists.

"That must be a great composer, Mozart?"

"Yes," he said and smiled, but not enough to reproach me. I can see now that he was, in between classes and presidential duties, studying Froebel and Pestalozzi before making the first translation into English of *De Anima* by Swedenborg, the great authority on the soul.

It seemed as if we were taught nothing. I do not think Maud (my nearest sister in age) was taught the piano at all. Today she is a dean of the American College of Organists and a recognized composer. I certainly had no more than a few months here and there. But we were set on the double piano bench beside my father or beside each other, before our feet could touch the pedals, to do what we could in the symphonies, Mozart, Haydn, Beethoven. My little hands would often come out scratched with the vigor of the composer's thundering chords. But oh! The gulps of glory!

There were other great memories in that parlor when the Choral Society [which my father brought up, as it were, out of the cornfields around Urbana] would meet for rehearsals. That Choral Society lived and breathed around him at the piano. His profound belief that everyone, any one, could do the fine things desired just by diligence and faith brought more than adequate tenor arias, and soprano recitatives, out of the homes and shops of Urbana. And what didn't they sing! Liszt's *Missa Solemnis,* Haydn's *Creation,* Mendelssohn's *Elijah,* and, always at Christmas, the *Messiah* of Handel . . . I have tender memories of my mother's lovely voice in the alto recitatives of the *Messiah.* The Society went in a body to take part in the biannual Cincinnati May Festivals.

In the parlor, also, I began a series of madonnas, in lead pencil, before I was ten, a complete picture with attendant angels every Sunday afternoon, in the big armchair by the front window.

For schoolwork we children were set around the long table in the schoolroom looking out over the croquet lawn between the fruit trees, with the white plaster Psyche standing at the end of the paths on her Greek pedestal. With eyes often on these things we learned from our German governess reading, writing, and arithmetic in German, with lovely fairy tales and bits of poetry. My father, not so long away from Tubingen University and the old German towns, carried what he could of their sentiment into the remodeling of the frame house we lived in—the carved newel posts, the mottoed fireplaces, and the oriel window on the stairs—and into our family life, the habit of walking in the country as a family for evening enjoyment. The German we read was high German, but our talk was often interspersed with low German, as his had been as a student.

My father, Frank Sewall, born in Bath, Maine, was richly gifted, highly educated in this country and in Europe. Called when a very young man to take a little institution of learning in Urbana, Ohio, which had been founded by a few ardent Swedenborgians like himself, and make it into the university which the state of Ohio had been inspired to charter. One can understand his zeal, almost his flashing exuberance. His liveliness was not only of physical energy, but a kind of beaming answer to everybody. His provision for his gifted little girls was to make sure to them that vibrating doctrine that "man truly lives for the first time when he perceives that he lives from the Lord." [Swedenborg, *Arcana Coelestia* paragraph 2196]. From his own delight in such worship, his thoughts were alive, his affections were alive, and so prolific there seemed to be no way to stop their happy overflowing. Such influences in Urbana made heavenly seedbeds in our young minds, as is plainly shown to be my father's intention in his book, *The Angel of the State.*

He had these things in mind in the selection of the Rev. Orson L. Barler for the head of the girls' school. This man is my first remembered teacher beyond my father. And it was the same sphere of spiritual awakening with assurances of order from inmost loves, through thoughts, into deeds. Anything beautiful could be done. To make this simple and useful was his purpose in the school.

In the first teaching away from home, Mr. Barler quieted perhaps some of my enthusiasms by what might be called study, though I am afraid I never really studied. We made excursions into botany; we began to read Latin. We came into geometry; but all of this was more or less swallowed up in an inner glory of meanings from the Bible, even from overhearing Spenser's *Faerie Queen* as the class just ahead of me recited; and it was expressed in cherubic forms I could not help drawing on the blackboard around my sums. These delinquencies were tolerated under the doctrinal principles of Urbana University.

John Singer Sargent.
*The Daughters
of Edward Darley Boit.*
Oil on canvas,
87⅝×87⅜ in., 1882.
Museum of Fine Arts,
Boston.
Gift of Mary Louisa Boit,
Julia Overing Boit,
Jane Hubbard Boit,
and Florence D. Boit
in memory
of their father,
Edward Darley Boit.

Mr. Barler, like my father, thought spiritually—that is, from causes, not facts. The fact of preserving our spiritual life while adapting us to the world was met by the knowledge that "one degree or form could not suffice to give life to anything, much less to give life to man. There must be forms in series, one interior to another, that a thing or being may come into existence and subsist [the discrete degree]; and there must also be extension, growth and development in each of the several planes of life [continuous degrees]." These are the profound steps on which I left my childhood.

We read Cicero and Virgil with my father. I believe he was not a good teacher of the language. He loved too much to give it instead of getting it out of us. I felt the resounding power of the text and could read the splendor of the Ideas. We went through the "Georgics" but the lasting grip of the construction I never mastered, another delinquency. I think he intended to take us into Greek, but something happened. Meanwhile the overflowing of the "spiritual love of uses derived from intellectual things" [Swedenborg] kept the whole family busy working out ideas. I wrote and produced plays with little sisters helping. Maud set Longfellow ballads to music. My mother made a chalk portrait of the five of us standing together, but something injured the head of Maud so that it had to be cut out and replaced. The impression of her tearful earnestness as she covered the scar and kept the lovely little head made a strong urgency to conquer despair grow in me. I have used it since.

Frank Sewall found Urbana University a good school waiting hesitant before its charter name. He left it a university offering classes from kindergarten to the bachelor of arts degree, through girls' school, boys' grammar school, young ladies' institute and college. He made it alive with the graceful appendages of the Minerva Literary Society, the Principia Club, the Morris Natural History Society, even the Latine, a book of witty, charming, and skillful Latin plays, many of which he wrote himself. These clubs, including the Choral Society, with their regular public meetings and their contests, their frequent chamber concerts and oratorios, and their cultural overflow combined with the style he gave everything he touched, made the university the real life of the town. The approach of a different spirit cut him off. He felt those in control were seeking an expedient for what we now call a realistic viewpoint, which generally means more fact and less truth. He announced the fulfillment of the $50,000 endowment which he had labored to gather, and then he resigned. Immediately he accepted a call from the Glasgow New-Church Society, and we sailed for Scotland.

We took my mother's guitar with us. Entering the gray fog of solemn Glasgow was a prelude to three years, from my sixteenth to nineteenth years, of European life and travel. I entered the Glasgow School of Art, Maud was put under a violin teacher, and the little girls were put in school. With the enjoyment of everything from the bagpipe beggars under our window to the seventeenth-century cathedral, we stepped into all the rich phases of city life—the orchestra, the great choral society, the conversaziones at the art gallery, the Ruskin Society, and the Browning Society, in which my father took an ardent part. These things sank deep into our young sensitivities and certainly expanded those continuous degrees which Mr. Barler had spoken of in our spiritual instruction. Underlying it all was the devout simplicity of the Swedenborgian group, meeting in a hall while the church was under contemplation. Despite the distinction of my handsome father, there may have been something, shall I say "rural" about us, unconfined? I am not sure what it was, but we never seemed exactly in the middle of the pavement. We are so yet.

In the heavy paneled dining room of our Glasgow apartment, my father carried on the education of Maud and myself over and above our school and practicing hours. There we read Gibbon's *Decline and Fall of the Roman Empire,* all of it. We dipped into the English philosophers, Hobbes, Butler, Hume, and Bacon—enough to stretch that "continuous degree" of a spiritual estimate of the Roman Utilitarian and the Stoic. Certain it was, we began to think. I have a feeling the Browning and Ruskin hindered this, though. I read *The Ring and the Book* with real joy.

I painted an oil portrait of Maud with her violin in the dining room: my first portrait. During our two winters there and the summer travels in England and in sparkling Edinburgh, and on the braes and around the lochs, how we found time—what with sketching and walking—to devour the English novels, I do not know, but we read almost all of Dickens, Thackeray, and much of Scott. I was even delighted in, though yet unappreciative of, Shelley. His un-Christianism hurt me even then. We also read Green's *History of the English People,* some Shakespeare, and the Lake poets as we dawdled down the lanes around Nab Cottage.

London left practically no impression on me but of the British Museum, where I was more alive than anywhere else in England or Scotland. There I met the Greeks, and their sunshine has possessed me ever since. With my newly acquired training from the art school, I made some drawings.

My father left the plans for the church building in Glasgow well under way, and a united and happy society where we had found one torn with schism. Then in the spring we drifted along to France. We did not travel as well-to-do people, never very comfortably, but under the skill of an artist in life. Whatever became of the rest of the baggage, the guitar traveled with us in the coaches. This gave us music at our journey's end. No matter what our shelter, knowing Italy, Germany, and France well from his student days, my father led us down many bypaths—we, from our inner habitations, were always immediately at home as soon as we arrived; attentive and ready. . . . Up went the sketches, out came the little library, and a place was found for the Bible and the Psalm books. That inner dwelling which it was my father's mission to erect wherever he went in the university-at-large, church societies, or his daughters' minds, may be called: the large upper room furnished which the Lord Jesus had commanded his disciples to find for Him. He was continually "making it ready."[1]

In the doctrinal class we older girls began reading *Divine Love and Wisdom.* I took Swedenborg mostly for granted then, even such sentences as *Arcana Coelestia* 162 "All the laws of truth and rectitude flow from the celestial principle or from the order of the celestial man" seemed very natural expressions of a truism to me. Only in looking back can I understand what they did for the perpetual sunniness in which we went about the world. Rainy days were wonderful, more so if a little chilly, needing inventions for comfort. Huddled together we could chuckle more and read better. Almost a disappointment to have the sun come out! And the book always in hand, the one business of the day! What beautiful rostrums we chose, always a view to be selected and faced first, no matter what the seat. That, when outdoors, was generally under some broad oak on the old sward of Switzerland or balanced carefully on a fallen column or well-head in Italy. We read Schiller around Interlaken and Zurich, *Maid of Orleans, William Tell, The Robbers,* of course in German.

The Sunday worship, wherever we were, was read and even chanted in full, where we sat decorously in our largest bedroom in whatever *wirthaus* or *pensione.* I remember particularly the celebration of the Holy Supper as he served it to us on a cold Easter morning in Siena while we knelt on the stone pavement of our room. He had an ever-present deep urgency to be led by the Lord and this accounted for the apparent security in which he made decisions.

Just why we spent so little time in France—not more than a month, I believe—I do not know. Frank Sewall had loved France, especially around St. Amand where, as a young assistant in making the index to Swedenborg in French, he had lived with M. Le Boys des Guays. And Paris he had delighted in as a traveling student. But now only the little Swedenborgian society there really held us. It might have been with me in mind that our weeks in Paris were spent in the great palaces and gardens, some evenings at the opera, some in society among the Swedenborgian friends, but no dallying as in other cities among the people on the bridges and in odd corners of history. Certain it is that he passed by the finest school in the world in silence and took his little flock to Florence. Driving over the St. Gotthard Pass in an open victoria, with three horses tandem, in the strong hands of a green-coated and feathered driver, we descended through the lake country to Florence, where we set up housekeeping in a suite of rooms, dependent mainly on sunlight for warmth, on Via Gino Capprone. The Duomo dominated the end of the street.

Nine months in Italy! How can the gold of it be counted? The language we learned readily enough from the handsome contadina who waited on us and from the markets and piazzas; also from the gentle signorina who was engaged to take charge of Maidy, Ray, and

Victorian
Home Schooling

Bess; also from the friendship of the little Swedenborgian group around Signor Scocia, all of whom met in our salotte for the Sunday services; chiefly, of course, from the easy conversation of my father everywhere as we rambled the whole length and breadth of the Val d'Arno.

The sharp change from German Switzerland was impressive. Not many weeks ago we had been among the saber-scarred faces of the students, young men proud of their duel marks. Here lyric gentleness seemed to flow in language and smiled in operatic resourcefulness. The domination that Greek art had taken over me in London and even in Paris was, strange to say, obliterated in Florence, its natural second home. The intense individualism of every city and village, the beauty of line and its utter expressiveness whether in manuscript, fresco, or in bas-relief, or up-leaping towers, required very different attention. The painted differences between the thirteenth and the fourteenth century seen in almost every corner exercised more intellectual insinuation over us than had the hoarded castles of indoor culture farther north. It may have been only the captivation of the freely visible—the color and feel of parchment, of velvet silver-clasped bindings, the pink and gold of Fra Angelico over the doors, the marble slabs hand-finished down to the bevel on the pavement, not an inch of it machine work, the liberality of beauty on the street that taught us so kindly. We became immersed in the republic, and devoted courtiers of the Medici. We used the spirit of Castiglione's *Cortegiano,* sometimes setting our plays and developing our evening gracefully around it. We took up cause after cause of church and the people, Savonarola, Michelangelo, ardently upholding and easily leaving one or the other for the next enticement.

I painted copies incessantly in the Pitti and Uffizi, in the cloister of San Marco and in the Accademia. In Florence and her precincts, we read her history and her relations to her great ones coming and going between her palaces and Rome, chiefly in the charming *Sketches and Studies in Italy and Greece* by J.A. Symonds. But of course the chief reading was Dante, begun at once in Italian. We read the *Vita Nuova,* and completed the first two great books of the *Divina Commedia* and part of the *Paradiso.* In the *Vita Nuova,* we learned by heart some of the sonnets, chiefly the *tanto gentile,* and set ourselves the contest of translating it to preserve the first beat without losing the pentameter.

My father was watching the world around him and working on literary studies of his own which appeared soon after in America, his beautiful little books, *The New Renaissance, Dante and Swedenborg, The New Metaphysics,* etc., the overflow and atmosphere of which he shed around his companioning daughters. He also made notable translations of Carducci, a poet of rising importance then, the first to be published in this country. In the English construction of these poems, he often admitted me as a consultant. We read in Florence Hermann Grim's *MichelAngelo,* also his *Life of Goethe*. We read the Greek tragedies for the first time. We prepared ourselves for Rome.

There I came under the magnificence of the serene Raphael, which to me has never been disturbed. And there I met the late chiaroscuro and the sixteenth century [the Cinque–Cento]. It seems to me we did little reading in Rome, and journeyed up the coast to Pisa and Milan. On our way to Venice we read the whole of Faust. Venice was too beautiful to see to admit of reading.

In the villages of the Tyrol we read *Hermann and Dorothea*. Also in Germany after leaving Weimar and still in the spell of Goethe, we read his *Gotz von Berlichingen*. We settled near the door of Wagner's Bayreuth theater for a while and became engrossed in *Parsifal* and *Siegfried*. Maud taught us the dramatic motifs from the little parlor organ in our boarding house, and we practiced them walking through the meadow to the performance. In Dresden, the great orchestra met us again, the whole of the *Niebelungen Ring;* all the Beethoven symphonies poured out to us, sitting on the terrace above the river. Strange to say, in Munich I began to come under the spell of the Venetian school, especially Mantegna. In Holland I came into the depths of Rembrandt and was entirely conquered by oil color and its profundities.

While in Switzerland, my father received a visit from a distinguished gentleman, John Hitz, of the Swedenborgian Society in Washington, D.C. He came especially to bring the invitation to my father to take up his pastoral life among them. My father accepted and left our brilliant and happy activities to become again the inspired preacher and leader, building another beautiful church.

The furniture of the home in Urbana arrived at the little house in Washington on Riggs Place, and in the small upper library, packed with bookcases and sunshine, I continued my reading with my father. I also painted a portrait of my two youngest sisters, in a style reminiscent of the Cinque–Cento. With the same thrift and delight that had characterized our study abroad, we interspersed the reading with art and music and the enjoyment of fine society. Among these was my father's delightful intercourse with the Society for Philosophical Enquiry, where he let me sit and listen, the Sophocles Club, the Literary Society, old and honorable groups of culture. My sisters' lovely voices led us to musical homes and with Maud's entrance into the Georgetown Orchestra, to precious associates. Finally my establishment in a studio of my own seemed to be the opening of a career in painting. I was twenty years old.

Our reading in the sun-baked little library included Taine's *History of English Literature* and Plato, dialogue after dialogue; Lecky's *History of European Morals,* and the partaking with my father in the intellectual marvel of Heredia's sonnets while he translated them, beautifully published soon after by Small, Maynard and Company in Boston. But the chief element in my mental growth was a real reading of Swedenborg, and even yet so superficial.

Then came the interruption for which it seems I had been prepared, the change of my career in art. A scholarly old man of the world, Howard Helmick, a distinguished painter fresh from his Academie des Beaux Arts associates in Paris returned to America to end his days here. I met him on the stairs going up to my studio. I invited him in proudly to show him my work. Before he left I was in tears, not of sorrow, but of joy, although he told me that everything I had done in color and in painting was wrong, that I was seeing without truth and delighting in it. My father, who had thought everything I had done was right, submitted to my verdict to give up my studio and my career, and go out to Georgetown to study with Mr. Helmick. He had intended taking no pupils, but he accepted me. I went out to him in Georgetown, receiving the drastic training of the Beaux Arts, pretty steadily for ten years. I began exhibiting, and painted many portraits, chiefly those of my father and of my mother. These were painted with the new knowledge Mr. Helmick had given me.

ALICE ARCHER SEWALL, the eldest daughter of the Reverend and Mrs. Frank Sewall, lived in Urbana, Ohio, until she was sixteen and returned there when she was twenty-nine as the wife of John H. James. In the interval she studied painting at the Glasgow School of Art, with Howard Helmick in Washington, D.C., and exhibited in juried shows. Today she is remembered primarily as a portraitist and as the founder of the Urbana Movement, an adult-education organization and art school that flourished in the 1930s and 1940s. ALICE B. SKINNER, a psychologist who focuses on the study of women's lives, is working on a biography of Mrs. James.

PART II

Learning Styles

Climbing Trees

I'd like to know
Why I climb trees.
It's hard on the knuckles,
It's hard on the knees,
It's hard on the sneakers and the jerseys and the jeans.
It would never do for Presidents or Congressmen or Queens.
But I can be a sailor, or I can be a scout.
I can see down to the corner from my top look-out.
I can see a grizzly coming from a quarter-mile away
(That's Mr. Potts the postman). On a sunny day
I can see Mrs. Possidente hanging out the wash,
And Mr. Wiseman weeding his tomatoes and his squash.
And they don't see me, and the birds won't tell
For I keep their nest a secret both from Emily and Bill.
I can't think why I do it, though I think very hard,
But we *do* have a maple tree in our backyard.

—JULIA RANDALL

FROMMEs
KALENDER

ZV BEZIEHEN DVRCH ALLE
BVCH=V=PAPIERHANDLVNGEN

LITH. ANST. A. BERGER WIEN 8.

M. GARRETT BAUMAN

When the Birds Meet Again

AS I RUSHED THROUGH THE STUDENT UNION toward my office, I noticed a heavy-set woman bending deep into the trash bins. That was not unusual. Five or six regulars—mostly shabby men—daily scoured the campus trash for beverage cans, redeemable for a nickel each.

But when the woman straightened and dropped two cans into her bag, the lumpy figure focused into Beatrice, a forty-five-year-old woman in one of my Advanced Comp classes. She had straight, grey hair and a broad, vacant face. By this, the third week of class, I'd realized she was a capable, sensitive student. I hesitated to address her. Being caught raiding the trash by her professor would be embarrassing. But if I edged away, I would shame her with my shame. She wore her usual thin sweatshirt and baggy jeans. A crowd of younger students thronged past in pre-torn sweatshirts and designer jeans, and a few administrators in their don't-touch-me grey suits sniffed at her with disapproval.

When she glimpsed me, her sagging face brightened. "Professor!"

"Hello," I said as casually as I could.

"I collect refund cans between classes," she said. "Bus fare. It's amazing what people can afford to throw away." We sidled out of the milling crowd—and its stares. Professors are not supposed to chat with campus bag people. "It's kind of wonderful, actually. I come to class each day with no cash in my purse—not a penny! But I scrounge lunch money and bus fare before I leave. It's just waiting for me every day!" When I asked what would happen if she did not find enough

Opposite:
Koloman Moser.
Frommes Kalender.
Lithograph, printed in color, 37⅜×24⁹⁄₁₆ in., 1903. The Museum of Modern Art, New York. Given anonymously. Photograph ©2001 The Museum of Modern Art.

cans, she laughed. "They just keep coming. What you need is always there if you're willing to look."

"Well," I said, "You know where my office is if you ever need bus fare." Bea did come to my office each week, but never for money. At first we discussed assignments, but we soon gave up that pretense. She would shuffle into my office and close the door, and we would chase her life around the four walls for an hour. She had a wonderful life, she said. She and her husband had owned an old house in the city and some land in the country where they planned to build a cozy cabin some day. Then, two years ago, James died. "I love him so much," she told me. "I miss him terribly. I still have the land—Oh, that sounds so empty! It used to be 'we' have the land."

She said, "If you'd met James, you might think, there goes a typical ant from the factory. Seven-to-four every day. No education. No vocabulary. But not an ant! We would read and talk until four AM some nights. I'd be half asleep, and he'd say something so interesting, I'd snap awake for another hour. Just the two of us, warm in bed in our old rickety house. He had courage, too—in the steady things. Only a real man could go back to a factory day after day when he knew he had better in him. He'd never have made college. He'd be round when they wanted square, and triangles when they wanted round. But he kept his family going. Our daughter, Lark, is diabetic and has kidney problems. But those nights when Lark finally slept after a bad session, he'd write such beautiful books in the air. I read them with my eyes closed."

James's cancer collapsed her world. "He told me, 'Bea, buy some heroin off the street. Just enough so I can get there. I don't want the damn hospitals to get everything we have. It'll kill me twice if I leave you with nothing.'" She wept then, tears proudly unwiped. "To save funeral expenses, he wanted me to bury him at the farm. Dig a hole and dump him in, I suppose! How could I? He was my hero. I don't know if I did right, but his last words were that he loved me." I offered the same cliché-sympathy most people do to the inconsolable. She waved the words away. "Oh, I still love him. He's inside me now. It hasn't changed one little bit." I simply nodded, a mute witness, as many teachers are, to secrets of the heart.

But life had not finished with Bea. James had died two months before qualifying for his pension, and his medical coverage also expired then—just as Lark needed surgery. James's life insurance and selling the old house paid for his death and Lark's life. Bea limped by on social security benefits, but would lose that next year when her son turned eighteen. "That's why I'm in college," she said. "I have to make something of myself by then."

"You *are* something now," I said.

"Not to the grocery store or phone company." She laughed. "Or the hospitals." And the laugh subsided. Her daughter was fragile, losing ground. I urged Bea to try welfare and Medicaid. She said they demanded too much. It was easier to gather cans. "I'm too old to jump through hoops to prove I need money. I told the social worker to look in my room, my refrigerator, if she thought I had hidden treasure."

She did submit to the bureaucracy to get her college tuition paid. She said she would go crazy without that. Nor could she exist without her land. To sell it for a few thousand dollars would be to sell her husband and children. That land could support her children's dreams if not her own. The cabin would be built someday. To her, it was already real enough to keep out rain.

One day Bea told me Lark had insisted on moving out of Bea's apartment so *she* could collect public assistance and spare her mother. "'Mom,' she told me, 'I can do this for you. You can still see me every day.' I just cried. I know what the system will do to her. They're so mean and cold-hearted, and she's so good, so sweet!"

Most people under such pressure become incapable of studying. But Bea flourished. Perhaps school distracted her grief or was a way of taking James to college at last. In any case, it was more than the need to get a degree to support herself. Day after day, her sagging face with the joyous memories, the tired mind crammed with ideas, the hurt, sympathetic heart filled my class. She clipped newspaper articles and chased ideas down twisting alleys until they surrendered. She questioned other students and the authors we read to wring the last drop of truth from them. When someone made a stupid remark or offered a half-truth, she politely stepped around it in silence. It was only bright nickels she wanted. Bus fare.

I recall one discussion of an essay by Loren Eisely, in which the young scientist captured a wild hawk for a zoo but had regrets and released it because he pitied the hawk's mate soaring and screeching high above. "I was so glad somebody does things like that," Bea said. "It was beautiful."

A young man in class objected. "What's one more hawk? It would live longer in a zoo anyway. I'm sure he caught another instead."

Bea said, "What counts is the moment when the birds meet again in the blue sky. It doesn't matter if the hawks die or if the world explodes. You have to live for those shiny moments."

The class loved her. Once she announced that a man had tried to pick her up on the bus all week. "He wants to take me to a movie and a bar. Me! And he shaves and wears a sports coat. Must have been drunk." Bea giggled.

The class urged her to date him. One boy offered to trail her as a spy in case the man tried anything. Bea laughed. After class I asked if she had dated since James's death. She smiled. "I'm married! It's just that he's dead."

She often wrote extra "therapy" pages. Five to ten pages at a time, some interspersed with drawings. After a few batches, I suggested she revise and preserve them. What I did not tell her was that I hoped assembling a little book might put James to rest and help her to move on. That was the proper goal, I suppose, to help her value herself for who she was now, alone, a person who should not be tied to a dead man. But my ulterior motive made me feel like a traitor.

She leaped ferociously at the project. Pages waited under my door or were thrown at me in the hall between classes, snapshots and letters clipped to them. She rewrote everything. The writing that was simply work for most students filled her hours and mind. Finding the right description to evoke a memory of a family night around a campfire under August stars was life itself to her. She drew pictures, labored with fine penmanship, and hand-sewed the pages into a book. When I suggested she type it to look professional, she smiled. "You don't type love letters."

She drew a rough-framed cabin window to fill the cover page, so I could not tell if I were looking in or looking out. Each chapter had drawings of stumps, chipmunks, a weathered fence or other rural things. She wrote about a hobbling, one-eyed dog they adopted, breaking ground for a garden, camping during a foggy week when crows landed on their tent. It was unrefined and intimately personal, as raw and tender as she was. A writer reveals her or himself truly no matter what disguises we try. But she wanted no disguises, only a faithful recreation of her life. She wrote of the happy times, the nights under covers planning paradise. Burning vines that set a field afire, playing a flute on the hillside, Lark at age twelve running through the meadow grass. She resurrected and embraced it all.

One day she said, "It's done."

I was proud of her. Her writing was wonderful. She learned economy, visualized through details instead of burying emotion under abstractions. But was her work done without bringing it to the present? I said, "What about James's illness and—"

"I don't need to remember the rest. This book is my life. The rest isn't." I stared skeptically, and she insisted she did not need to write the rest down. "I'm reminded of it every day I put on these clothes and wash in that rusty sink. Writing this book brought back so much happiness. You'll never know how good it feels." Why should I argue? We could do worse than spend our time redeeming bad memories for a few silver ones.

After our final class of the term, she dropped into my office to thank me for spending extra time with her. "If it hadn't been for you," she said, "I'd have forgotten so much. I have more of him to remember now."

I nodded, knowing that she had been doing it herself anyway, that I simply supplied an ear and eye to receive it. I felt lucky to have had her on my roster and to have had her want to confide in me. She set down her half-filled bag of cans. "I wrote a song this weekend," she said, squirming like a child anxious to reveal a secret. "Would you like to—"

"Sure," I said. "Let's see it."

"Well, I thought I might sing it to you."

Although the situation was too eerie for me to recall the words— she sang from memory—I can still hear her voice. For a big woman's, it was thin, but sweet and delicate. Flute-like or birdlike perhaps. It was the woman inside who sang to me that day, the beautiful, forever young and loved woman. Hands folded in her lap like a gospel singer, Bea gazed in my eyes and smiled during her singing. At first I glanced away in a bit of a fluster, then managed to accept her eyes. It was youth, joy and lost paradise she sang to me that afternoon. It was a safe place to leave James and Lark and those forever shiny plans that would never be. I have seldom felt so humble and unworthy. I hope when I face misery or death that I can be as joyful for all I have had in my life.

Halfway through her song, Bea's eyes glistened. Still she smiled and sang. She was beautiful in her frumpy clothes. Her puffy, creased face radiated. Disease, poverty and death could not snuff out that light. If hope and value exist, I saw them that day. I bent my head at the end and nodded. She sniffed, fumbled for her handkerchief and blew her nose. Then she rose wordlessly and shuffled out, the black bag clinking on the floor behind her like a pet dog.

M. GARRETT BAUMAN teaches at Monroe Community College in Rochester, New York. He is the author of *Ideas and Details* (Harcourt) and of essays and fiction in many publications.

DON ROSE AND MIKE TAYLOR

Suffer Fools Gladly

**Are you ignorant?
What a question!
Ignorance is shared
by all mortals.**

**The appropriate
question
is not really
whether
you are ignorant
but how you
feel about
your
ignorance.**

"GIVE ME A BREAK — I'M JUST A TRAINEE."

You can be in denial
about it.
You can assume
the persona
of a "know it all."
Or you can be
the kind
of person
of whom it is said,
"You can't tell
him or her
anything."

You can acknowledge
your ignorance
with a regretful sigh
or
you can appreciate it
for its blessings.

But what does
it mean
to be ignorant?
If someone
were to ask you
if you know much,
it would be hard
to answer
because
it is a relative thing.

Compared to some, you know a great deal.
Before the question can be answered,
it must be established what you are
to compare your knowledge to.

Compare what you know
to what you do not know.
Consider this carefully
and then say whether you know much.
Can you appreciate
that there is no end to knowledge?

"HE'S THE DUMMY, MOTHER, I'M JUST PLAIN IGNORANT."

If you make the comparison correctly,
you will give the appropriate answer
that your knowledge is comparatively nothing.
No matter who you are, you are ignorant.

"HOW DO YOU *FEEL* ABOUT YOUR IGNORANCE?"

**How does it feel to be ignorant?
It can be a thrilling thing to realize
that knowledge
is inexhaustible.**

**According to Swedenborg,
the angels of heaven speak
of a Temple of Wisdom.
Not everyone can see that temple,
say the angels, "No one sees it
who believes himself wise enough,
and still less he who believes
himself wise from himself."**
(*Apocalypse Revealed,* paragraph 875)

"LET'S FACE IT—SOME HALOS SHINE BRIGHTER THAN OTHERS."

Says Swedenborg, "It is genuine wisdom for a person
to see from the light of heaven
that what he knows,
understands,
and is wise in,
is so little in comparison
with what he does not know and understand,
and in which he is not wise,
as to be like a drop to the ocean."
(*True Christianity*, paragraph 387)

There is a feeling of awe called "the Holiness of Ignorance." In *Heavenly Secrets* it is said, "One who does not acknowledge that there are infinite things with which he is not acquainted, beyond those with which he is acquainted, cannot be in the holiness of ignorance in which there are angels."
(*Heavenly Secrets,* paragraph 1557)

"MY ADVICE ?... NEXT TIME, USE THE ELEVATOR."

The holiness of ignorance does not consist in being more ignorant than others, but in the acknowledgement that of ourselves we know nothing and that the things we do not know are infinite in comparison with those we do know."
(*Heavenly Secrets,* paragraph 1557)

"DON'T WORRY, BUDDY, I'VE GOT CABLE."

You and I should not be surprised
and certainly not discouraged
when we come upon things we do not
as yet understand.

Rather
should we
be grateful
that we can
always see
a little
more.

DONALD L. ROSE is a grandfather who edits a monthly journal of Swedenborg studies. MIKE TAYLOR lives in San Francisco. His cartoons regularly appear in *Tricycle, Writers Chronicle,* and *Modern Haiku.*

ERROL MILLER

Most Poets Draw

Doing nothing right comes
naturally. Life has taught me little.
Morning will find me burning coffee
and drawing circles that
never meet.

Smelling fish, I put hunger
first. Rushing out to a mirage,
I become disenchanted. So I write
that down. What did I say?

My life is a circle. I
have never met me. What is it
that I do not know? I've been to
barber shops. By now, most
people know everything.

ERROL MILLER, a frequent contributor to the Chrysalis Reader, has been
published in *American Poetry Review, Hollins Critic,* and *Maryland Review.*
He was a featured artist in the *2000 Poet's Market.* His latest book is
Magnolia Hall (Pavement Saw Press).

ROBERT M. PECK

Juggling Your Smarts

Fernand Leger.
La Parade.
Gouache on off-white
paper, 1954.
The Harvard University
Art Museums.
Gift of Mr. and Mrs. Jose
Luis Sert.

AS THE EDUCATION DIRECTOR OF THE INTERNATIONAL JUGGLERS
ASSOCIATION, I periodically conduct seminars where I get to invite
conventional businessmen to "think outside the briefcase." I do this
by teaching them how to juggle in slow motion with colorful nylon
scarves. Even the more buttoned-down types soon drop about
twelve pounds of stress. More importantly, they discover that juggling is an ideal activity to get both mind and body working in har-

mony. When we move on to beanbags, they soon realize that "Keeping all the balls in the air" is simultaneously a poignant symbol of time-management and a versatile spiritual metaphor for maintaining a focused yet flexible balance of attention.

Juggling also provides a tangible model of Howard Gardner's Multiple Intelligences Theory in action, a head–hand–eye coordination, which requires and reinforces right- and left-brain synergy. The ability to keep more objects in the air than you have hands taps diverse intelligences (logical, visual–spatial, bodily–kinesthetic, musical, etc.). The result is that often the people who pride themselves on being quick studies wind up having to learn from colleagues who surprise everyone, including themselves, by how quickly they catch on. It's in this new hierarchy that participants are most receptive to seeing how much it would humanize our work environments and increase the quality of our collaborations, if we would simply reframe the question, "How smart are you?" to the more inclusive, "How are you smart?"

Multiple Intelligences Theory basically boils down to the fact that there are many different kinds of "smarts." Some folks are book smart; some are people smart; some are art smart, and some, if they've been watching too much of *The Simpsons,* are Bart-smart! Yet for most of our lives, we're inculcated with the belief that cognitive smarts that can be translated into an IQ score are the true barometer of a person's intelligence. I'm convinced this does us all a grave disservice. A more inclusive definition of intelligence would go a long way toward making our schooling more democratic and could play a pivotal role in humanizing our work environments.

Starting with our grade-school experiences, imagine if, instead of focusing on the traditional 3 R's "readin', writin' and 'rithematic," our report cards emphasized the 3 T's: Teamwork, Tolerance and Tenacity? The former lend themselves more readily to quantifiable measurement. But just because the ability to calculate sums or spell vocabulary words can be easily and rapidly assessed, this shouldn't inflate their importance, especially since so much of what makes for a successful learning environment entails qualities that are *immeasurably* important. It may be frustrating that we don't have the instruments to gauge someone's imagination, caring, or leadership quickly or accurately. But in terms of real-life value, the kind of book-smarts that enable a person to score high in traditional testing situations pales before people-smarts like empathic communication and visionary thinking.

To claim that higher scores on paper and pencil tests prove that a child whose strong suit is cognitive thinking is smarter than a student who's gifted in art or music is just plain intellectual bigotry.

Teaching isn't about taking exams . . . it's about transmitting enthusiasm. And if anyone wants to gauge the level of learning going on in a classroom, the best test . . . is zest!

Of course if Gardner had simply called his theory "Multiple Talents," no one would have raised an eyebrow. But he deliberately wanted to challenge the prevailing academic notion that "specials" like drawing, drama, or dance were merely talents, whose serious development shouldn't receive equal emphasis in the classroom. Through research and compelling scholarship, Gardner elucidated the symbol systems and other cognitive related "vocabulary" common to both the performing and creative arts, in effect validating the intelligence that is creatively expressed in mediums ranging from music to watercolors.

He also broke down so-called "people-smarts" into two distinct but complementary components. The first he terms interpersonal intelligence, how we understand and relate to others. The second he distinguishes as intrapersonal intelligence, how well we know and understand ourselves. The former is one which typically gets addressed in the classroom via cooperative learning endeavors such as group projects. The latter is still largely overlooked and often grossly underestimated. Again, it's as if what counts is determined by what can be counted by external measures. Yet, most of what frees us to make good use of our gifts is the direct result of our ability to know who we are and to be clear about our priorities.

By taking a more rounded view, classroom practices that foster reflection and self-inquiry level the playing field and offer a more inclusive view of what deserves to be thought of as intelligence. In addition to interpersonal and intrapersonal intelligences as well as linguistic and logical (verbal and math), Gardner's diverse list includes visual spatial, bodily kinesthetic, musical, and naturalist intelligences.

The results are schools that are more able to teach 'em because the teachers are more able to reach 'em by gearing their lessons to their students' strengths. When it's hard for squirmy Johnny to sit still during math, such teaching integrates into the lesson something that entices and draws upon Johnny's 'attention assets'. Those hot buttons of interest, be they art or music or games, that if used as an entry point, grab Johnny's attention and help to hold and harness his full concentration. For instance, instead of drilling him on what the principal exports of Zanzibar* are, why not tap into Johnny's musical intelligence by incorporating the information into a song? Likewise cultural customs come alive when they are conveyed

---

*The author gratefully acknowledges being inspired in his choice of country by the pertinent story/song of the same name by the gifted singer/songwriter/storyteller, Bill Harley.

through a traditional tribal rain dance. And best of all, such a rhythmic, sensory rich approach plays to his strengths and makes the classroom a place that positively reinforces his self-confidence. All of which goes a long way toward the ultimate aim of any educator—to instill a lifelong love of learning.

Multiple Intelligences theory put into classroom practice restores the root meaning of the word educate (from the Latin *educare*), which means to lead out or to draw forth. Human brains are so infinitely intelligent that effective education isn't so much how to instruct as how to invite.

From this perspective, even our mistakes trigger valuable incentives for deepening our interpersonal intelligence. For example, when learning to juggle, if we condition ourselves to see the inevitable D.R.O.P. as simply a Daring Release Of Pressure, a Determined Reinforcer Of Persistence, or a Dramatic Rejection Of Perfection, we're able to keep our balance even when we fail. An equanimity that allows us to respond to an errant toss with a lightheartedness that puts anyone watching immediately at ease.

The nucleus out of which these kinds of psychological and sociological synergies occur is intrapersonal intelligence. How we deal with our juggling triumphs and tribulations provides powerful springboards for both self-discovery and self-reflection. What we learn about ourselves, our assets and limitations, teaches us a great deal about our character and directly impacts our self-confidence.

Both our aspirations and our challenges prove fertile grounds for developing creative (often cooperative) problem-solving competencies. Indeed, it's often only when fallibility strikes that fortune smiles and deepens our reserves of both resiliency and resourcefulness. Surely if "necessity is the mother of invention," failure is the father.

With a little diligence, people soon begin to experience some success with their juggling as well. And once they master the basic progression, continuing to hone their juggling skills leads them to experience a raft of other fringe benefits—including the rewards of delayed gratification, the importance of goal setting, the power of sequential learning, and the necessity of being able to laugh at and learn from our imperfections. (Hey, If you're gonna defy gravity, you gotta stay light!)

In addition to the way juggling concretely reinforces patience, persistence, and empathy, it also positively affects overall coordination, with often markedly improved fine-motor skills. As if that's not enough, past participants have proudly reported that learning to juggle is a truly balanced and genuinely centering form of meditation. Most also come away with a real feeling of accomplishment and a much deeper understanding of the "secret" behind the apparent paradox of relaxed concentration.

"Keeping all the balls in the air" demonstrates and deepens our understanding of how several different intelligences can be consciously intertwined. The act of juggling playfully engages people's heads, hands, and hearts in a way that simultaneously develops and deepens their understanding of integrated learning and higher-order thinking.

Both metaphorically and practically, the process of learning to juggle reminds us of the ups and downs we all experience in our social and cognitive development. By respectfully recognizing each other's unique gifts, honoring our intellectual diversity, and playing to people's strengths, we bring out the best in each other. The results are schools which instill a lifelong love of learning and workplaces where greater personal fulfillment and heightened job satisfaction lead to a win–win personally and professionally for both the employers and employees.

From classroom to boardroom to living room, a broader view of what constitutes intelligence would benefit all concerned. And much as a practical application of Multiple Intelligences Theory helps make curriculum come alive, I'm convinced it could also play a pivotal role in making our work environments foster our best thinking and most satisfying collaborations.

Honoring the fact that there are many ways to be smart isn't so much a right-brainer or a left-brainer as it is a NO-BRAINER! Certainly for anyone on a spiritual path, cultivating a more inclusive definition of intelligence is part and parcel of maintaining a healthy respect for individual differences and embracing the fullest measure of our humanity.

ROBERT PECK is the founder and C.E.A. (Creative Education Advocate) of Zestworks—a speaking, training, and consulting firm which believes that "the best test is zest!" After graduating from the University of Pennsylvania (Phi Beta Kappa) and Ringling Brother's Clown College ("Magna Cum Looney!") Rob's eclectic career has taken him from being the recipient of the International Jugglers Association's Excellence in Education Award and a featured guest on Donahue to being the keynote speaker at major corporate events.

MICHAEL J. LICHTENSTEIN

Exchange Student

Middle-School Teachers Educate an Academic Physician

AS A PHYSICIAN MEMBER OF A MEDICAL SCHOOL FACULTY, I never expected to be working with teachers in public schools. Yet it happened, and my life and teaching style have been transformed for the better.

My recollections of medical school in the mid-1970s include sitting in lecture halls for hours. Our professors barraged us with slides containing the information thought necessary to learn the lexicon of medicine—the building blocks for becoming a competent physician. Some of my classmates chose not to attend these classes, able to study in their apartments and glean what they needed from the texts and comprehensive handouts that accompanied the lectures. In some medical schools, large lectures remain poorly attended—the class designates scribes—students selected to attend the specific session, take careful legible notes, and then reproduce them for their classmates. This was my first inkling that there were different learning styles, although I was too focused on my own survival to worry about what others were doing around me at the time.

Clinical work and residency training taught me that I learned best on my feet. This is a fundamentally different way of learning. When I take care of patients and read about their problems, these actions leave indelible memories that form a growing experiential foundation of knowledge. Yet, moving on to the next stage of my career in the mid-1980s, an Assistant Professor of Medicine, I forgot this when it came to teaching others. The models of my faculty col-

Opposite:
Jack Quigley.
*Stopping to Ask
a Swamp Mahogany
for Directions.*
Photograph, 1998.

leagues placed an emphasis on being authoritative. The compelling image for me was the successful physician–scientist in starched white lab coat, stepping up to the lectern with a carousel full of blue-ozalid National-Institutes-of-Health-style slides. This person delivers a tour-de-force talk showing that no one understands the topic better than he does.

True or not, that was my reality, and that's what I wanted to be. Never mind that the medical students would probably send a scribe to record my words. My primary focus was going to be on writing grants and conducting research that would make a meaningful difference to the health of people. "Teaching poorly could hurt you, but teaching well won't help you," was an academic reality among junior faculty on the tenure track. I intended to model my path on the senior professors and leaders in my department—if it worked for them, why shouldn't it work for me?

One of the tickets academic physicians punch on their path to success is getting involved with the work of their respective professional organizations. This raises your profile and garners national recognition—a commodity examined closely by promotion and tenure committees. Early in my career, I chose to work with the Southern Section of the American Federation for Clinical Research (AFCR then, now the American Federation for Medical Research [AFMR]). A small plurality elected me to office at the regional level, which gave me a seat on the National AFCR Council.

The 1992 National AFCR Council Meeting was to change my life, although I did not know it at the time. Lynn Morrison, the AFCR Washington lobbyist, exhorted our group of medical scientists to get out of our blinkered paths and get involved with public-school science education. Lynn argued, compellingly, that improving public-school science education would be a strategic political move to increase our visibility with Congress. I kept my mouth shut but rolled my eyes, thinking, "Right . . . we're supposed to compete for grants, conduct and publish research, teach medical students, residents, and fellows, and take care of patients. Now you want us to get involved with public-school education, too? No thanks, that's someone else's problem." This was too far from our mission and lives as far as I was concerned.

Back home in San Antonio, Arlan Richardson, a biologist investigating molecular mechanisms of aging, had succeeded in putting together a National-Institute-on-Aging-sponsored program for incoming medical students designed to expose them to geriatrics and gerontology before they started their formal curriculum. In late spring 1993, one of the medical students withdrew from Arlan's program. "What do you think we should do with this stipend?" he asked me. Before I had a chance to think, the words "Why don't we get a middle-school science teacher in here from the community?" blurted out of my mouth. I regretted those words the instant I said them, but it was too late.

The middle-school science teacher turned out to be Linda Pruski, an extraordinarily talented magician who was interested in absolutely everything. In many respects, teachers are magicians in that they bring together children from varied backgrounds and abilities and guide their learning in a collective environment. Linda spent the summer at our Health Science Center squirreling around the labs, attending my clinics, going with me on home visits, spending time on the clinical research center, and digging in the library. All the time she was thinking about middle-school science requirements in Texas and gathering material to use in her classroom that fall. It was an absolutely delightful experience for her and for me—it certainly went beyond the realm of ordinary expectations. By the end of summer, Linda compiled a large stack of background material, lab exercises, and visuals that could teach required curricular concepts with examples from gerontology.

Linda called this stack of material 'gerimeandering.' Although clever, I balked at the negative associations between aging, meandering, and gerrymandering. Linda had seen a number of vigorous elders with me, and we agreed to search for a more constructive framework for teaching materials dealing with aging. We also agreed that this initial experience working together wasn't sufficient. There are parallels between Linda's work as a middle-school teacher and my work as a geriatrician. Middle-school teachers often work in interdisciplinary teams and take responsibility for a subset of students—in this way they can compare notes and team-teach—reinforcing their lessons by complementary methods. Geriatricians also have to work in interdisciplinary teams to do an adequate job of meeting the social and emotional needs of their patients and families. So we left the fall with a resolve to get Linda's middle-school academic team into the Health Science Center the following summer.

Summer 1994 saw a full team of middle-school teachers (science, math, reading, social studies, and English) work with basic and clinical scientists from the Health Science Center to create new instructional materials about aging. Our process was first to brainstorm ideas. The teachers then used the Health Science Center resources to research and draft lesson plans. Finally, they presented their ideas and activities to our faculty for feedback. This iterative process taught me much about the presentation of information—especially the value of creating lessons that are active and inquiry-

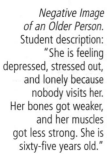

*Negative Image
of an Older Person.*
Student description:
"She is feeling
depressed, stressed out,
and lonely because
nobody visits her.
Her bones got weaker,
and her muscles
got less strong. She is
sixty-five years old."

based rather than formally pedagogic. From this process, the *Positively Aging* teaching materials were born.

In creating the *Positively Aging* lessons, the teachers and faculty provided integrated instructional materials that facilitate essential curricular element instruction by using examples from geriatrics and gerontology. It is challenging to make space in a crowded curriculum for new content. For example, students need to learn the essential scientific concept of *density,* so we developed lab exercises that use bone-density measurement to teach this concept. From bone density, we linked lessons that teach bone biology and maintenance of bone health across the life span. We labeled the use of gerontology examples to teach curricular elements *Stealth Gerontology* as a way to infuse content about aging into the school. Our purpose was not to change what is taught, but to provide lessons that effectively teach the necessary concepts.

Working together, the teams of teachers and scientists also designed the *Positively Aging* teaching materials to help students make critical, life-determining decisions for extending and enhancing their own lives. This goal focuses on health promotion and disease prevention. When middle school students are asked in an open-ended way about aging, they express many neutral (e.g. 'wrinkles', 'gray hair') or negative (e.g., 'slow,' 'can't hear') stereotypes. Rarely do students envision these changes occurring in themselves, nor do they associate any of these changes to age-related conditions. This disconnect provides opportunities for health promotion education.

*Neutral Image
of an Older Person.*
Student description:
"This woman is
thinking about getting
a magazine off the
coffee table and reading
it. She is going to drink
some coffee. She has
gray hair, wrinkles, and
little hands and feet.
She is seventy-two."

Our faculty interactions with school teachers allowed them to take knowledge about age-related diseases and health promotion from the Health Science Center and format it in a way that works in their classrooms for their students.

The process of creating new lesson plans for the *Positively Aging* teaching materials evolved and grew—from the initial four units in 1994 the scope increased to its present format of twelve interdisciplinary units covering topics as diverse as diabetes, sensory impairment, cognitive function, and cross-cultural comparisons. In 1997, the National Institutes of Health granted our team a Science Education Partnership Award (SEPA) to evaluate the effectiveness of the teaching materials. Using a combination of qualitative and quantitative techniques, we demonstrated that the *Positively Aging* teaching materials move middle-school students to a more positive view of elders. Now, with a second SEPA grant, our team is transferring our print material to the World Wide Web. We want to disseminate our classroom-ready lesson plans—created by teachers for teachers—as widely as possible <www.positivelyaging.uthscsa.edu>.

I wake up every morning amazed that I am intensely involved with public-school educational research as a member of a medical-school faculty. But my wonder and disbelief are not the points of this essay. Working with public-school teachers has profoundly changed my style and methods of teaching for the better. I have yet to find the words that adequately describe my feelings about this transformation. When I think about it, I am pleased that I am capable of, less threatened by, welcoming of, and seeking change. One of my per-

*Positive Image
of an Older Person.*
Student description:
"This is my grandmother
who I call Nana.
She is seventy-two.
She is speed walking
with her dog, Inga. She
is feeling great and in
shape. She is a little bit
more wrinkled, but
looks healthier than me.
She taught me how to
eat right and stay in
shape."

sonal aphorisms is, "Change is inevitable—how happy you are is determined by your ability to adapt to change." So I am happier.

I am the school teachers' student and have learned more from them than they will ever know. That's one of the conundrums of teaching; you never know where you will have your biggest impact—many days you feel like you have no impact at all.

So how has my teaching evolved? I do not lecture any more and I rarely make slides. I do not want to get up in front of a group of people and tell them how much I know about a narrow area of medicine. I do not want to be regarded as an expert—that is a recipe for becoming stale and staid.

Proactively, I do want to have conversations with people and exchange ideas. I do want to understand where my trainees are in their personal education and help them explore new areas of information. I do want to know where my trainees' areas of knowledge are deeper than mine so that I can learn from them. I do want to model inquiry and begin and end student contact with questioning—if it's a one-on-one encounter at the bedside, a small seminar, or a more formal classroom, it should all begin and end with questioning. I do want to learn actively, integrating new knowledge into the care of my patients, comparing and contrasting the written dogma with the experience of illness.

Because of the school teachers, I am much more relaxed when I am in an instructional environment. In class, I envision a community of learners that shares knowledge. I am no longer scared of the gaps in my education, but seek others to help me gain greater understanding. No longer do I envy the knowledge or skills of others but rather seek learning alliances to achieve shared goals with my teacher colleagues. I want to improve the quality of teachers' professional development and students' education in our public schools.

MICHAEL LICHTENSTEIN is a professor of medicine and practicing geriatrician at the University of Texas Health Science Center at San Antonio. He believes equal access to, and participation in, quality educational programs are keys to eliminating health disparities. His program is supported by a Science Education Partnership Award (SEPA R25-RR-12369) from the National Center for Research Resources, National Institute on Aging, and the National Institute for Dental and Cranio-facial Research. Dr. Lichtenstein is also supported by the National Center for Research Resources grant MO1-RR-01346 for the Frederic C. Bartter General Clinical Research Center.

STUART AROTSKY

Europa

Glaring at the gray-ice ridges,
watching the ripples, the scrollwork,
as if these patterns across Europa
are the impressions of god's fingers
packing this clump of ice into a globe
as a child composes a snowball
before tossing it to the cosmic winds.

Science has marked this world
as the brightest of reflective bodies
within our harmony of spheres.
But what draws every inquisitive eye
is the hint of an ocean
                    beneath its barren surface.

I know these shattered sheets
from Jupiter's neighbor.
In winter, puddles along a road's margins
became an inducement to my boots.
I would fracture the plate-like bodies
drenching my toes
                    in the briefest plunge
                                        into polar liquid
leaving the plates to freeze again
          in a pattern repeated upon the sky.

Now science longs to dredge
below this glacial land
to ensure that the elixir of life
                    lurks within.
            Curiosity spurs us on
        to penetrate the enigmatic shell,
to embrace this mysterious, eighth sea
in the same way a child plays upon the world
                            for the same reason,
                                    to know.

STUART AROTSKY holds an undergraduate degree in journalism and a master's degree in education. He is currently teaching fifth-grade students in his hometown of West Haven. In between writing poetry and lesson plans, he is working on a science-fiction novel.

HEATHER TAYLOR

Body Surfing

I STAND, BODY FACING WEST, head craning east, waiting for the dawn of another sizable wave. Squinting through the salt and sun, I lick my lips, tasting that unique stickiness as the ocean dries on my mouth. "There's one!" I hear the adolescents call out on the left. "Here it comes . . . Get ready, get ready . . . Woohoo! . . ." and they're off like dolphins, rolling waves roaring them along on the hiss of salt foam. They body surf with an expertise I cannot yet understand.

I see the next roll of white approach. I push off on the sandy bottom. Leaving the outer layers of calloused feet behind, I'm right in the curl of the wave. buoyed only temporarily before dropped in the soup again to look on as that fifteen-year-old rockets off ahead of me. Rats! What am I missing? Mary Jane says, "You've got to kick as you go, propel yourself . . . keep the energy going, I think."

Another wave. This time I watch the pro youth start before the wave even hits. And he is zooming, arms folded on his back, calmly surveying the world as he rushes toward shore. Aha! I think. So that's it—I have to start sooner. Hmmm. When the next wave comes, I'm already kicking ahead, prepared to be pushed along. For about four seconds, it works. I can actually feel the power underneath me as I move like a new species of sea mammal. For the next hour-and-a-half, I play in the waves, trying to learn to feel the right moment, to change one thing at a time, the timing, the push-off, the position, the effort—to achieve the longest ride on the soft-surging water. The process of learning to body surf is like many other efforts. It involves starting at one point, trying things out, thinking about how it went, then forming a new concept or new question or fortifying the previous ones with new experience.

I remember being taught these steps, maybe in elementary school, maybe in junior high. This is what a "scientist" does: hypothesize, experiment, analyze, report. After memorizing these steps, we performed an experiment that thousands of others had performed before (perhaps the good ol' baking soda and vinegar volcano trick . . . Or maybe finding the caloric value of foods using Bunsen burners and graphs . . .), achieving the same results and graded to show our successful venture into the "scientists'" world. It certainly seemed like a superficial window into what it means to think scientifically. It was sort of like pretending or play acting rather than exercising one's intellect.

Ellen Day Hale.
Willow Whistle.
Engraving on buff wove
paper $12^3/_4 \times 8^7/_{16}$ in.,
1888.
Pennsylvania Academy
of the Fine Arts.
Purchased with funds
from the Henry D. Gilpin
Fund.

We learned, perhaps by accident or perhaps through careful encouragement of our teachers and guides, that some people are naturally scientists, and some are artists, some natural social workers. . . . We learned to focus on what we did well, spurred on by the well-meaning guidance counselor. What an important skill, to know what you are good at. We learned simultaneously the unspoken flip side of that shiny success-track coin: don't waste your time on what you're not the best at. In the competitive world of adults that lies ahead, lingering in a less-than-achievable skill was a sure way to fail—to flip burgers, to pump gas, even if that made you happy, you certainly couldn't suggest you might earn your living that way. And so we left science to the scientists, art to the artists, and knew what we couldn't do.

How is it that so many of us have learned to define ourselves as unscientific (or mathematically stunted or artistically bereft)? It seems as though our culture has taken to the trend of specializing. We no longer care with our own hands for most attributes of our lives. We buy the bread someone else has baked, drive the car to someone else to fix, resolve our conflicts through someone else's litigating process, and perhaps spend our days focusing on a tiny part of the everyday business to share with others who seek our expertise. In the specialist mode, we forget our larger abilities, we forget that we are capable and diverse thinkers and problem solvers, and we learn to let someone else figure it out.

As an educator, I wonder how I can help to break down the limits of a specialized society. How can I help children to develop as independent and critical learners? The answer comes one spring morning as my class and I are out in the woods. I am watching Caleb as he tries to maneuver a way-too-big branch into position for his animal home. First he tries to break it with his hands, then by holding one end in the air and jumping on the other end. Growing frustrated, but still determined, he grabs another shorter stick and begins whacking it against the other, trying to chop it. Again he is faced with the unyielding mammoth branch. He flings the impromptu ax to the ground and stands for a moment with his head down, his hands on his hips. Several moments pass. Then, he is back into action, asking a neighbor to help him wedge the branch between two tree trunks. He heaves against the trunks of the trees, and snaps the branch off, with a bit of a shock and a stumble, yet glowing in his triumph.

Caleb has just run through the evolution of humankind in the last ten minutes . . . using tools, using levers, working in community . . . and he had the opportunity to make these discoveries through uninterrupted play. I could have stepped in, either to break the branch myself or to show him how to prop it against the trunks, but then I wonder if he would have learned that he can figure things out himself, that he can create different ways to solve problems. Would he learn that he is a trustworthy source of ideas and a capable builder and thinker?

I still feel intrigued by the question of what it means to "know" something. Once we have "knowledge," do we know what to do with it? How to apply it to our life and needs? How do we identify knowledge? How do we assess knowledge? Surely there is no way to show Caleb's learning of that morning in the no. 2-pencil-darkened ovals of computerized sheets. Watching Caleb in the woods reminds me that learning is simply what children DO! They cannot help themselves; they are learning all the time, and even if we do our damnedest to get in their way, they still learn. The idea that we need to categorize, quantify, and qualify their learning at times seems completely absurd to me. When is the last time any of us adults learned something new, actively pursued a new skill that left us feeling completely foreign to our bodies or language or usual state—like learning to juggle or fly an airplane . . . or body surf? Children are in this state constantly, learning the alphabet, grappling with the concept of time and clocks, getting small fingers to tie the right kind of knot that can later be untied to let out little feet. I think we forget what hard work this is, what tension can rest in the body, what stress there can be in hoping to achieve, to gain success. Every day, all day, what miracles they perform!

I received a report for a new six-year-old student from another school district. They sent a packet of information about her. What was in the packet? Her absentee record and standardized test scores. What did this tell me about her? Something about the relationship of her aptitude to her abilities? Something about her skills in language versus math? Yes, but what about the other important things I would need to know about how she learns: how she functions in a group, how she separates from a parent in the morning, how she organizes her knowledge, and whether she can extrapolate yet? Does she enjoy school? What really gets her jazzed about learning?

When we teach to only one dimension of the total beings of children, we grow one-dimensional thinkers. We cultivate independent and isolated specialists. I think there must be a better way. Through providing opportunities in play, in conversation, in action, we need to develop all the facets of young learners. We need to provide them with the knowledge and confidence that they are able to succeed at whatever they apply themselves, and that they can learn from and with others without being dependent on others to figure it all out. Therein lies the key to relevant education.

And then we too relearn the lessons of our youth, relearn that we can figure it out if we let ourselves stand with our hands on our hips, let ourselves crash against the next wave. If we grace ourselves with permission to try and try again, even at what we are "not that good at," we learn volumes, absolute volumes.

HEATHER TAYLOR is a writer, painter, and teacher living in southeastern Vermont. She has eight years' experience in teaching five- to eight-year-olds. She is the associate editor for *Connect,* a magazine of teachers' innovations for K–8 science and mathematics.

ANDREW FLAXMAN

The Opened "I"

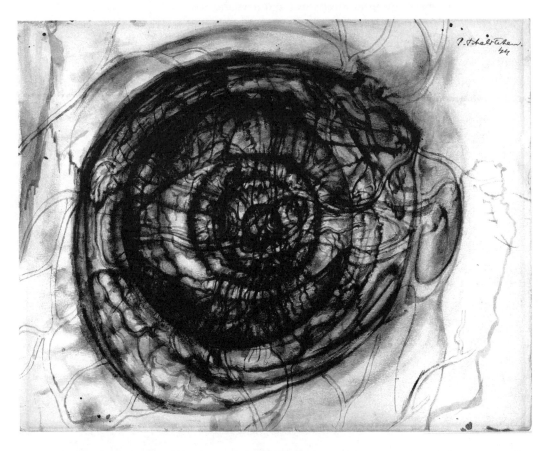

Pavel Tchelitchew.
The Eye: Study for
"Flowers of Sight."
Black ink, watercolor,
charcoal on cream paper,
1944, 14⁷⁄₁₆×11⅜ in.
Philadelphia Museum
of Art: The Henry
P. McIlhenny Collection
in memory of
Frances P. McIlhenny.
1986-26-352.

FOR HUNDREDS OF YEARS, THROUGHOUT THE ANCIENT WORLD, kings
and commoners traveled to Delphi to ask the Oracle of Apollo about
the right course of action—whether to make war or seek peace,
whether to marry one person or another, for advice on watershed
questions. These seekers of wisdom brought rich offerings to the god
and were sent on their way by the priests with the Oracle's riddling
answers. But over the Delphic sanctuary's entrance was the admoni-
tion *Know Thyself*, suggesting that the true oracle lies within!

Answers to the great human questions, public and private, are so
often found not beyond us, but rather through a journey inward of
our seeking spirit. The crucial importance of developing self-knowledge was pointed out in the Hebraic Talmud, which says, *We do not*

see things the way they are; we see things the way we are. In other words, we grind the lenses with which we see the world.

What exactly is this self we need to know? Civilized people today generally see themselves in very physical and psychological–religious dimensions but often remain unaware of further aspects of their being. How do we develop deeper insight so that we can recognize and integrate our intuition, imagination, and inspiration into our conscious everyday lives, leading to better self-understanding?

To develop our inner gifts in this way requires the crucial discovery of the "open eye." To this knowledge is where a liberal-arts education would ideally lead us, but so rarely does. The conventional approach to the humanities often consists of rote teaching, memory training, and problem solving. Opening the "inner eye" requires experiencing the "I" as an integrated whole, an ego (Latin for "I") that balances thinking, feeling, and willing. Increased mastery of this integrative process leads to the ability to distinguish between true intuition and mere whim, between inspiration and empty abstract thought, between creative imagination and disconnected fantasy.

Such personal development may very well go against the flow of conventional Western thought. For five-hundred years Western civilization has developed through the exploration and conquest of the "outer" world, a progress accelerated by our scientifically inclined materialistic philosophy. The world thus viewed becomes separated from our inner being. And yet, if one looks more deeply, imagination, inspiration, and intuition—all spiritual, integrative processes—are at the core of our scientific and cultural discoveries. Einstein said that he valued his ability to speculate and fantasize above his mathematical skill. The new physics is based on doing away with the attitude that "I am here, and it's out there." The observed, say the new physicists studying sub-atomic phenomena, is always changed by the observer.

Despite the new physics, so much of the way we currently think and live is structured by dualism (binary thinking), the commonplace way of thinking in terms of either/or, bad/good, inner/outer. Whether our faith is in science, progress, God, human nature, or government, our present outlook is often confined to dualities. Only enhanced self-knowledge enables us to transcend the temporary illusion of duality and one-sided materialism. An experience of opening the "I" breaks through to the integration of head, heart, and creativity that is the core of all reality—the "patterns of organic energy" with which the Zen masters of ancient China were concerned.

Where do we find constructive help in this difficult journey into ourselves? We can turn to the great artists, writers, thinkers, statesmen, and scientists throughout history who have communicated their heightened sense of awareness through their lives' work. Through artistic forms and significant deeds, their work can awaken us to a higher view of ourselves. Their examples can make clear that we have more than five senses. We can go beyond our material senses to deeper levels of cognition. We all have dormant organs of finer perception, the capabilities cultivated by leading human beings throughout history. If we can understand and absorb those insights, we can ourselves participate more completely in the great creative force that drives humankind forward and upward. It is only a matter of learning how to "see better" as the loyal Earl of Kent implores King Lear. In other examples:

- Rembrandt shows us the way to personal integration through his transforming treatment of light and shadow.
- Jung teaches us how recognizing and accepting the bad as well as the good parts of ourselves can increase our energy and our sense of wholeness.
- Lincoln helps us to reconcile steadfastness and flexibility, idealism, and realism.
- Idries Shah teaches how the humor of Sufi tales can be a valuable key for self-awareness.
- Mozart offers music to synthesize our hearts, bodies, and minds.
- Shakespeare helps us tap the profound source of wisdom within each of us.
- Einstein's theory of relativity leads to the understanding of how important it is to know the spiritual self in order to regain a sense of the absolute.
- William Blake illustrates the process of achieving union with the spiritual world.
- The myth of Herakles demonstrates that throughout the centuries there has been an evolution of self-conscious awareness parallel to the Darwinian evolution of mankind's physical being.
- Plato helps us to understand the true nature of love beyond sexuality, friendship, loyalty, and romance.
- Dostoevsky deepens our sense of what real freedom is about.
- Rudolf Steiner shows us that economic life can be healthy only if we have a greatly increased knowledge of ourselves.

The new liberal-arts curricula at many universities includes selections from non-Western, female, and minority sources, reflecting, perhaps, a recognition that the classical approach to the humanities has its limitations. But the quest for universal relevance in education will not be actualized until education is founded on the conscious development of dormant cognitive capabilities leading to a deeper understanding of ourselves and the human condition. The development of the whole human being must be fostered: an education of the mind, the heart, and the will.

RECOGNITION OF THE NEED TO REVISE traditional core curricula of the humanities is not a recent phenomenon. Amos Comenius (1592–1670), the great Moravian educator, was one of the first to modernize the classical university system. His textbook, *The Visible World*, was the first work in which pictures were as important as the text. Determined to translate into common-sense what previously had existed as classical tradition, he wrote that he wished to construct a temple of wisdom that would serve as a sacred edifice for education similar to the Temple of Solomon. Comenius's temple was to house a school of universal wisdom, a workshop for attaining all of the skills necessary for life and the future.

Comenius advocated a comprehensive education taught in the vernacular. He promoted establishment of many more schools and universities. He was asked to design the curriculum for the newly established Harvard College but instead chose to organize Sweden's educational system. He pioneered the use of academic specialization but warned that if the spiritual foci were not emphasized, educational unity would be lost.

To help free today's student from traditional programming and to become more autonomous and creative, education needs to also focus on the universal aspects in the work and lives of creative individual, who have had a positive impact on civilizations. Literature, art, and music should be taught as tools for self-discovery rather than reduced to mere cultural entertainment or as a means to achieve grades. Memorization and intellectual emphasis can actually distract the student from engaging in a more subtle level of appreciation. Important insights are gained through questioning and reflection on how great issues bear upon our lives. Education becomes higher education when it develops positive mental and psychological attitudes that young adults can use for a lifetime. The heart of a liberal-arts "core" curricula should encompass:

- *Moments of inner tranquility:* that state of being wherein we are at peace with ourselves. By stepping aside from the turmoil of daily life with its incessant distractions, we obtain moments of inner tranquility that are a starting point for self-education about our actions and feelings.
- *Recognizing our feelings and then being able to detach from them.* This putting aside of one's likes and dislikes and seeking to examine *what is,* not what gratifies, leads to a state of

objective awareness different from the familiar personal and subjective condition.

- *Conscious objectivity* allows us to see things from different points of view and enables us to see some truth, purpose, and meaning even in attitudes and behavior we otherwise might find totally abhorrent. This ability does not make us lose our sense of judicious discrimination—on the contrary it enhances it as well as our understanding of the world.

- By *withholding and suspending judgment,* we keep our minds open to new discoveries. As soon as we judge, we limit our curiosity and thought. We are thus able to *understand* how often we have "thrown out the baby with the bath water." Disagreements, prejudice, and criticism often lead us to miss crucial insights that can enrich our lives.

- True open-mindedness and thoughtful objectivity lead to *learned ignorance* which overcomes intellectual arrogance and false pride. The more we learn, the more we understand how much we do not know.

Without unifying principles with which to appreciate the values in the liberal arts and to relate them to our lives, we can find ourselves knowing more and more about less and less. To gain the essence of classical knowledge, however, we must explore the world within us and experience a unifying love of education.

ANDREW FLAXMAN received a bachelor of arts degree from Princeton University and a master's degree in business administration at Rutgers University. After a successful career as an investment banker and stockbroker, he became concerned that our economic life seemed fraught with increasing selfishness, egotism, and lack of self-knowledge. Thus, for the past few decades he has become a publisher of self-educational products, a seminar organizer and director of Educate Yourself for Tomorrow, a spiritual self-study humanities program.

LORAINE CAMPBELL

Husband Number One

Balthus (Balthasar
Klossowski de Rola).
The Bernese Hat.
Oil on canvas,
1938–1939. The
Wadsworth Atheneum.
Museum of Art, Hartford.
The Ella Gallup Sumner
and Mary Catlin Sumner
Collection Fund.

WHEN I WAS SIXTEEN, a few days before report cards were due, I went
to Reno, stood in an office, and married a sailor.

There were no flowers or bells, no one threw rice, just tan window shades pulled halfway down, brown desks, and the ticking of
several typewriters. I stared at my long pink fingernails while a
Justice of the Peace asked us if we took each other to be a lawfully

wedded something or other. We both said, "I do," while the type-writers clicked. Then the Justice of the Peace said: "I now pronounce you man and wife, and that will be fifteen dollars please!" He smiled and shook my husband's hand, then waited, still smiling, while my husband fumbled around looking for his wallet. Suddenly I had a horrible thought: What if my new husband, of less than one minute doesn't have any money? I was in such a hurry to get married I forgot about that part. I pictured the Justice of the Peace, with his smile drooping, saying, "Sorry kids, it just won't take," and there I'd be, back in school. There I'd be, grounded every night in my room, memorizing the dates of the battles of the Civil War and studying my map of New Zealand. I began nibbling on the skin around my fingernails. Finally, my husband found his wallet and handed over the money; and the Justice of the Peace handed us a license with a big gold seal. I knew, even though the ink was still wet, that this piece of paper meant that all my problems were solved, and nobody could ever boss me around again.

"Oh, darling," I gushed, grabbing my brand-new husband and sinking my pink nails into his blue uniform. "I love you very, very much!"

We rented a room with plastic curtains and a bed that came out of the wall. The mattress sagged like a trough. We rolled into the center of it and spent the weekend there.

Early Monday morning, while it was still dark outside, my husband leaped out of bed and told me to wake up and get him some breakfast.

"And hurry!" he ordered. "I have to be at the base."

"But I don't know *how*," I whined, rubbing my eyes.

"You can fry an egg, can't you?" he shouted.

"Oh, sure," I said, grabbing one of our new pans and groping my way to the stove. I yawned and turned the flame all the way up. Then I cracked the eggs by hitting them together, and the yolks flew everywhere. Smoke billowed up, the pan turned black, and the eggs looked like lumps of charred glue.

"Don't you know you're supposed to use some goddamn oil?" my husband shouted. "And why is that flame so high?"

"Because you said to hurry," I whimpered, rubbing the smoke out of my eyes.

"Oh, just forget it," he yelled. "I'll eat my breakfast at the base."

He ran out the door, then turned around. "Don't forget to look for a job today," he said, coughing and rubbing his eyes.

"I won't. I mean, I will!" I said.

"So we can start saving for a house."

"I know. I will. I mean, I won't. Forget, I mean."

"Good!" He slammed the door, causing the pan to rattle against the stove.

I groped my way through the smoke and opened a window. Horns were honking in the street. I leaned out and yawned, watching everyone rushing around.

My husband's voice echoed in my head. "Save for a house"—a house?—wow, a house!

I shut the window and lay down on the bed. "Everyone's getting ready for school now," I thought. I pictured my friends, standing in front of their closets, trying to decide what to wear. Then they'll be picking up their report cards. I smiled, thinking of my gym teacher, who had grabbed me by the collar of my starched blue and white uniform, on (what I knew and she didn't) was my last day of school. She hissed into my face that she was giving me two F's on my report card. "One F just doesn't cover it!" she sneered.

I pictured all the girls lined up in alphabetical order reaching for their cards, and a blank space where I used to be. I could see that teacher with her jaw stuck out, standing there with a surprised look on her face and staring at both F's.

I smiled again, then suddenly realized that none of the kids knew that I was married!

I jumped up and hurried down the hall to a pay phone, dialing quickly.

"Is Lucy there?" I asked Lucy's mother.

"Yes, she is. But she's busy. She's getting ready for school. She's already late, and she doesn't have time to talk on the telephone in the mornings. I've told you that already."

"I know," I said. "But this is *really* important!"

"Hi," Lucy said a few minutes later. "Are you wearing a crinoline today?"

"No," I said. "I won't be there today, or ever again! I'm a married woman now!"

"You *what?*"

"I said, 'I'm a married woman now.' Oh, and I have my own pad, I mean apartment, now too. I can't talk very long, I have all of my housework to do."

"Your mother let you get married?"

"Well, not exactly. But there comes a time in life when your mother's opinions are obsolete!"

"Obso—gee—that's really nifty."

"You can come over after school if your mother says it's all right," I laughed. "Of course I'll have to know what time she wants you to be home. I wouldn't want you to miss getting your homework done." I laughed again.

"Oh, drop dead," Lucy cried, slamming her phone down. I stood there for a minute, staring at the pay phone, then fished around in my bathrobe pocket for another dime. Tossing the dime around, I tried to decide who else to call. It would be fun to tell a couple of the boys from school that I was now married, but it would be better if I could see their faces. I pictured myself meeting them, individually, exchanging a quick kiss, then lowering my voice and saying, "I have something I simply must tell you!" I tossed the dime around some more, then dropped it in my pocket and went back to my room. "I just don't seem to have anything in common with school children anymore," I told myself, before getting back into bed.

When I woke up, there was a beam of sunlight streaming through a gap in the plastic curtains. It hit me in the face. I sat up and looked at the clock. "English composition," I thought, "that's where I'd be, conjugating a bunch of dumb verbs, if I weren't—I'm married—you're married—he, she, it is married—hey, I better get up and get my housework done!"

I took the cellophane wrapper off our new broom and swept dust and little pieces of the linoleum floor into the hall. Then I tried washing the pan, but the water turned black and the pan didn't get any cleaner; so I slid it under the bed.

A few days later, I got a job in a lunch counter that was near all the banks and office buildings in town. There was no jukebox, no sailors, just a steady stream of businessmen on their coffee breaks or lunch hours. There was the constant crashing and banging of metal trays and porcelain cups and plates, and the continual scraping of meat and lettuce into garbage pails. The waitresses, including myself, all ran around screaming orders at the cooks, things like: "Hambone galloping, hold the fluff!" I longed for my old after-school carhopping job right away—paper dishes, servicemen throwing spit wads at me and Gogi Grant singing on the jukebox: "The wayward wind is a restless wind, a restless wind that yearns to wander."

LORAINE CAMPBELL began writing after years of being an amateur painter and reports that she has learned two key principles: keep it simple and stay close to the heart. Her stories have appeared in *Pulse, Papyrus, Works and Conversation, Grit, The Sun, Aim,* and *Writing for Our Lives,* as well as in the Chrysalis Reader.

PART III

School Days

The Whale Race

From Baja up to Glacier Bay,
St. Kitts to Labrador,
The whales are racing every one.
They shake the ocean floor.

Let San Francisco tremble,
Let Fundy stem its tide,
For all the whales are racing,
And Seas from side to side

Swing this-a-way, and that-a-way,
And so the waves are made,
On sand at Ocean City,
On stone at Portland Head.

Wherever waves are breaking
Or rolling tall and blue,
Leviathan, Leviathan
Is racing through.

—JULIA RANDALL

NAOMI GLADISH SMITH

"New-Church" Education

A Historical Perspective

This summary owes an immense debt to Richard R. Gladish's scholarly and carefully researched four-volume History of New Church* Education.[1] *Most of the information about the early schools presented here has been gleaned from Dr. Gladish's invaluable treatise.*

FROM THE DAYS IN LATE EIGHTEENTH-CENTURY LONDON when a little band of readers of Emanuel Swedenborg's visionary theology first met to worship together, an education based on Swedenborg's religious principles has been considered of paramount importance by many of his followers. Though Swedenborg himself never attempted to start a church—and, in fact, many who utilize his ideas have never joined a Swedenborgian church—several church organizations and many church societies were founded in the two centuries following his death in 1772.

Swedenborg often speaks of the 'New Church', stating that a new church is what is meant by the New Jerusalem of the Apocalypse. That heavenly city seen by John the apostle on the isle of Patmos symbolized a spiritual community that will exist in heaven and on earth, says Swedenborg. Its membership will acknowledge and worship the Lord alone, he says, and it will hold his word holy, will love divine truths, and reject faith separated from a life of loving usefulness.[2] Since those eighteenth-century days, various groups have founded organizations they have called 'New Church'; this article addresses the interest in, and support of, education by those organizations.

Opposite:
Oskar Schlemmer.
Bauhaus Stairway.
Oil on canvas,
63⁷/₈×45 in., 1932.
The Museum of Modern Art, New York.
Gift of Philip Johnson.
Photograph ©2001
The Museum of Modern Art, New York.

*In the nineteenth century most organized religious groups that adhered to Emanuel Swedenborg's theology were formally called *Church of the New Jerusalem.* Members of these groups often called their organization the *New Church,* and an individual member was often referred to as a *New Churchman. New Church* as an adjective is still used in some cases as a formal name for a Swedenborgian faith community.

WHILE IT IS UNIVERSALLY ACCEPTED that education is a preparation for adult life in this world, New-Church educators have long believed that education should prepare the student for spiritual life as well. Almost fifty years ago the Rt. Rev. Willard Pendleton wrote in *Foundations of New-Church Education* that "knowledge is not an end in itself; it is only a means by which man may acquire wisdom."[3] Bishop Pendleton further states, "the beginning of wisdom is the acknowledgement of the Lord," that knowledge of God is not intuitive, but like any other knowledge must be acquired by way of instruction. A primary axiom of New-Church education therefore is *instilling a true idea of God.*

The concept of *use* is another essential of that education: use being not only a person's occupation, but in the larger sense the good that person does throughout her or his life. "New-Church education is not merely a process of formal instruction," says Pendleton, ". . . it is an effort to direct the thought and affections of the child from self to use."

Since the establishment of that first Swedenborgian church in London some two hundred years ago, men and women have given of themselves and their substance to found schools that not only teach the truths found in Swedenborg's writings, but also teach secular subjects in the light of those concepts.

IN HISTORICAL PERSPECTIVE, the beginning of the organized 'New Church' also marks the beginning of the Industrial Revolution. It was a time when thousands of children whose parents worked in England's new mills and factories roamed the urban streets. As there was no national system of education, public spirited Englishmen soon realized (for very practical as well as a humanitarian reasons) that some form of schooling must be provided for the illiterate, undisciplined hoards. New-Churchmen were in the forefront of those who responded. They not only saw the necessity of providing schooling for these youngsters, but considered it a providential opportunity to teach the children Swedenborgian values and beliefs. Thus began a proliferation of New-Church Day Schools throughout England, schools that charged little or no tuition and over the years would educate more than six-thousand children.

The earliest mention of a school in which children were taught from a Swedenborgian perspective is of one conducted by a Mrs. Lowe in 1785 in a suburb of Manchester, but the first typical day school under the auspices of a New-Church group was the New-Church Free School founded in London in 1822 by the Rev. Thomas Goyder. By 1876 twenty-five New-Church schools had been established in England. With the advent of the National System of Education, however, surviving as a school that taught beliefs other than those of the state religion became more and more difficult, and by 1907 almost all these schools had been taken over by the government.

One that did remain was not a day school but the Emanuel College founded in London in 1845. Planned as a two-tiered institution with a lower school offering a New-Church education to boys and an upper level that provided a theological education for those who wished to become ministers, Emanuel College took a long time to get going and closed the lower school in 1884, but the theological school endured. It became The New-Church College, moving to Woodford Green in 1930, and then to Manchester in the 1970s. Today the school has about thirty part-time students, three of whom are working toward ordination. The college does not offer degrees as such but has a four-year course for those who wish to become ministers and a three-year course for 'auxiliary' ministers. It also offers Friday-to-Monday sessions both winter and summer for college-age students at Purley Chase, the New-Church Conference's meeting center.

THE SITUATION IN NINETEENTH-CENTURY UNITED STATES was quite different. Here, rather than performing a proselytizing function, early New-Church schools served primarily to educate children of New-Church members.

One of the first of these was on an Ohio farm near Steubenville, where in 1810 David Powell Sr. built the Powell Farm School for his twelve children. Interestingly, Powell felt forced to open the school because some of his neighbors threatened to withdraw their children from the local school if the 'Swedenborg children' were permitted to attend. Powell, who became a New-Church minister in 1817, was evidently an able teacher, for according to his son, David Powell Jr., the neighborhood children soon asked to attend, including some whose parents had voiced earlier objections to subjecting their offspring to the 'Swedenborg children' (Dr. Gladish quoting David Powell's *Autobiography*).

In 1836 two schools, one in Providence, Rhode Island, and one in Boston were founded under the auspices of New-Church societies. In 1838, the Swedenborgian Society in Bath, Maine, also established a school, and the following year one was started up in Abington, Massachusetts. In fact, though most lasted only a few years, between 1836 and 1866 a total of fifteen New-Church schools came into being. An exception to this lack of longevity was the Waltham New-Church School, begun in 1860 in Waltham, Massachusetts, with Edwin Gibbens as principal and the Rev. John Worcester as superintendent. This New-Church school continued for many years, becoming the Waltham School for Girls in 1911, then Chapel Hill

School in 1937 (though managed by the board of the New-Church Institute of Education, by this time it had few New-Church students). In 1971 it merged with a boys' school and became, as it remains today, Chapel Hill–Chauncy Hall, with no religious classes or affiliation.

Back in 1866 another long-lived school had been founded in Waltham. In response to the Rev. Thomas Worcester's call for a training school for New-Church ministers, the New-Church Theological School opened its doors. That first year it offered only a three-month summer session, but by 1870 it had students from Canada and Norway as well as from various parts of the United States. The school moved to Boston in 1878, then to Cambridge in 1888. In 1966 the school, by now called the Swedenborg School of Religion (SSR), moved to Newton, Massachusetts. The SSR developed a masters degree program in Swedenborgian studies and offered certificates in theological studies to laypersons as well as a four-year training program for the ministry. SSR is now transitioning to Berkeley, California, where, as the Swedenborgian House of Studies (SHS), it will affiliate with the Pacific School of Religion (PSR), one of the most prominent interdenominational theological schools west of the Mississippi. According to the Rev. James F. Lawrence, acting dean of SHS, the Swedenborgian Church regards this move as a "coming out of isolation." The future SHS will offer not only theological training, according to Lawrence, but in addition to continuing to offer lay programs, the school intends to provide correspondence courses and on-line courses to "a larger world of theological scholarship and spiritual seekers."

Another New-Church school that has had an exceptionally long existence is Urbana University, founded in 1850 at Urbana, Ohio. The university was the dream of the Rev. James Parke Stuart and Milo Williams, a New-Churchman who in 1850 and 1851 began a preparatory school for the proposed college with eighty-three boys and girls. Urbana University opened its doors in 1853 and by 1856 had 128 students. Until recently that was the high point of enrollment—the lowest being 1957 when it served just seven part-time students. Efforts at rejuvenation proved singularly successful, however, and today Urbana University has an enrollment of 1,350 and offers undergraduate degrees and a master's degree in education. Though few of today's faculty or students are members of Swedenborgian churches, the curriculum offers ten courses in religion. Lisa Oda–Fede of Urbana's communications office reports that one of these courses is titled "Swedenborg's Religious Thought" and that most of the religion courses there include some Swedenborgian concepts. The campus also houses a Johnny Appleseed museum honoring John

Chapman, a follower of Swedenborg's teachings. While traversing Pennsylvania, Ohio, and Indiana to sell seedlings from his nurseries, from 1807 to 1845, Chapman distributed chapters of Swedenborg's books to his customers and to anyone interested.

Among other schools founded during this early period of the Swedenborgian movement were the Foster Hill School, begun in 1854 near Cincinnati, and the Bartels School, which opened in Osage County, Kansas, in 1870 and closed only because the 1874 plague of grasshoppers caused the dispersal of the New-Church group that had founded it. Another Ohio institution that had a short, tempestuous life was the Mary Allen School of Glendale. This school, founded in 1891 with money left for that purpose by Mrs. Allen, a widow and former Latin teacher, was to fulfill a dream of Mrs. Allen and her husband, formed after they'd seen the success of the nearby New-Church Foster Hill School that functioned for sixteen years, until 1870.

Mrs. Allen and her husband envisioned not only a school, but a New-Church cultural center as well. And this is what happened—for awhile. Then came a rather spectacular court case that forced the school's closing when relatives seeking Mrs. Allen's inheritance attempted to prove that both Mary Allen and Swedenborg were insane. Ultimately the suit was unsuccessful and the school reopened as an orphans' home, but in 1898 the Glendale Swedenborgian Society voted to sell the property and to appropriate monies realized from its sale for other church uses.

ALTOGETHER, DURING THE PERIOD OF 1785 TO 1876, over fifty schools having some connection with the New Church sprang up in England and the United States. Though few of these lasted more than a handful of years, there was one on the horizon that would grow into a vital, dynamic educational system that thrived throughout the whole of the twentieth century and continues today.

The Academy started as a fundamentalist movement within the formal Swedenborgian organization in North America. A group whose primary interest was the education of children and young people, its members firmly accepted divine authority of the writings of Swedenborg. Over the years theological differences between the two groups increased to the extent that in 1876 a number of ministers and laymen, led by the Rev. William H. Benade, formed a separate entity, the Academy of the New Church, and also began a divinity school that was chartered by the state of Pennsylvania in 1877. In 1890 the General Church of Pennsylvania, the church body to which most Academy members belonged, separated itself from the original

North American conference of Swedenborgians. In 1895 the General Church and the Academy moved from Philadelphia to Bryn Athyn, a few miles beyond the city, and within thirteen years Bryn Athyn had become an educational center with a theological school, a college, a girls' seminary, a boys' school, and a coeducational elementary school. The General Church was not without its difficulties, however, which culminated in 1897 with the withdrawal of the entire church from Bishop Benade who had become extremely dictatorial following a stroke.

The first elementary school begun under Academy influence beyond Pennsylvania was the Immanuel Church School. Founded in Chicago in 1879, the school was primarily for young people but had weekly evening classes for adults. It was suspended in 1882 (possibly because of the Chicago riots), but resumed in 1886 and in 1895 removed to a Chicago suburb later named Glenview. Today Glenview has a pre-school program and the Immanuel Church School that teaches students from kindergarten through eighth grade. It also operates the Midwestern Academy, which offers a two-year half-time program for students in conjunction with the local public high school.

Next came an elementary school begun in 1885 at Pittsburgh, still in existence. Two Canadian schools, one begun in Kitchener, Ontario, in 1888, and one started in Toronto in 1890, today have a total of eighty students.

As might be expected, the largest elementary school in the General Church system is the Pennsylvania school begun in Philadelphia in 1894, which moved to Bryn Athyn. More recent elementary schools are: the Washington School started in Mitchellville, Maryland, in 1970, the Oak Arbor School begun in 1978 in Detroit, and a New-Church school that started the same year in Kempton, Pennsylvania.

In Bryn Athyn, the girls seminary, boys school, and Academy of the New Church college, begun in the late nineteenth century, have continued to flourish. Today the schools and the recently renamed Bryn Athyn College have a total of 400 students.

The Academy theological school continues to provide ministers for the General Church and offers post graduate education for lay men and women. Thirteen theologs were enrolled for the 2000–2001 year and fifteen lay men and women are in its master's degree program. Aside from all this formal education, for over a hundred years there have been Swedenborgian camps for teens and for families, the latest innovation being 'Eldergartens', week-long schools for senior citizens.

IT IS EVIDENT FROM THIS HISTORY that the emphasis on education begun in the eighteenth century continues today because of the strongly held desire of generations of New-Church men and women to pass on the life-affirming truths they have found in Swedenborg's thirty-some theological volumes.

This article would not be complete, however, without mentioning a further, critical motivation for promoting a distinctive New-Church education. This is the singularly Swedenborgian idea of 'remains' or 'remnants'. According to Swedenborg's *Heavenly Secrets* 'remains' are "everything good and true which the Lord instills into a person from earliest childhood through the final period of life."[4] And further, "[A person] is endowed with these states from earliest childhood, though that endowment gradually diminishes as he advances to adult life."[5] In another passage from the same work remnants are called celestial things that "flow in from the Lord" and are "implanted both independently of cognitions (knowledges) and together with cognitions. The implantation independently of cognitions occurs during infancy to childhood . . . whereas the implantation of them together with cognitions occurs after that, from childhood to adult life."[6] Teaching in a setting that recognizes God as the center of all life, therefore, is conducive to instilling those remains or remnants, in children especially but in seekers of all ages.

Today as in the past, many New-Church men and women believe this kind of education helps preserve the innocence of little children and provides young people the tools with which they can make choices that lead to a life of use on earth and in the eternity of heaven. They believe that it is an effective means to teach the ways of God.

Notes

1. Richard R. Gladish. *History of New Church Education: Education under English Conference of the New Jerusalem, 1785–1967; Education in North America in the Sphere of the General Convention of the New Jerusalem, 1800–1968; A History of the Day Schools of Church Societies of the General Church of the New Jerusalem, 1800–1972;* and *A History of the Academy of the New Church (from its beginnings to 1966)*. Unpublished doctoral dissertation (1967, 1968, 1973). Swedenborg Library, Bryn Athyn, Pennsylvania.
2. Emanuel Swedenborg. *Angelic Wisdom Concerning Divine Providence*. First published in Latin, Amsterdam, 1764. First English translation 1790. Current English translation, Swedenborg Foundation, West Chester, Pennsylvania, 1996. Paragraph 264.
3. Willard D. Pendleton. *The Foundations of New Church Education*. Rev. ed. The Academy Book Room, Bryn Athyn, Pennsylvania, 1960. p. 61, p. 65.
4. Emanuel Swedenborg. *Heavenly Secrets*. First published in Latin, London, 1749. First English translation, London, 1774. Current English translation, Swedenborg Foundation, West Chester, Pennsylvania, 1998. Paragraph 2280.
5. *Op. cit.* Paragraph 1738.
6. *Op. cit.* Paragraphs 1450 and 1451.

NAMOI GLADISH SMITH is a Chicago-area writer. She has written for various publications and has read many of her essays on 848, a local National Public Radio station program.

LANI WRIGHT

My Topographical Map of France

Asa Ames.
Phrenological Head.
Polychromed pine,
16⅜×13×7⅛ in.,
c. 1850.
American Folk Art
Museum, New York.
Bequest of Jeanette
Virgin. 1981.24.1

When this doll's head
was painted,
phrenology dictated that
each part of the brain
housed a separate
mental faculty.
How much more than
geography gets packed
into each small head?
And how does it
all meld into
one smoothly-
functioning person?

OH, THE VAST MYSTERIES OF ELEMENTARY SCHOOL with its labyrinth of shiny corridors, echoing bathrooms, damp locker rooms, and unprotected playgrounds where anything could happen, and did, and probably still does. It is fourth grade. We are studying France. Miss Millman is directing as we make topographical 3-D maps out of sculpted Plaster of Paris on top of large squares of cardboard pre-cut from orange cartons. The heady aroma of plaster of Paris and oranges wraps itself around me like a curtain of concentration. Of course, I wonder as I pinch the nipples of Alps in a long line along the border of Switzerland, if we were making 3-D maps of some other country, say Spain, would we be using plaster of Madrid? But I do not raise my hand and ask Miss Millman, though I want to, because I have recently received a U meaning unsatisfactory, a word I can't pronounce well but understand the meaning of in the "works well alone" square on my report card, so my mother has told me that I should not talk to my neighbors, and I should not ask too many questions, and I should just concentrate on doing my assigned work. I begin making the smaller nipples that are the Pyrenees along the border of Spain. I have decided to paint a gold star to show the capital city of Paris. I know that in France they pronounce it Par-ee, as my mother has told me when she sings about wild times in Gay Paree and practices her cancan kicks at the stove while frying hamburgers for supper. I start to tell this to Polly Mahuta, my neighbor, but then I remember that I am concentrating on my assigned work and decide I will just wait and impress Miss Millman with it after class.

Frances Mead, who sits next to me, is large for fourth grade. She reminds me of a Kewpie doll, a big, soft rubbery Kewpie doll with crimped hair. She has this naked feel to her even though she always wears babyish dresses with Peter Pan collars with little satin bows in the front where the two scallops met. Frances has raised her hand, and now Miss Millman is giving her permission to go to the girl's room. As soon as she's gone, I edge my way over to her desk to check out her Plaster-of-Paris France. I note with satisfaction that she is way behind and hasn't put a single mountain in place yet. I think I am probably ready to start painting in the major rivers—the Rhone, the Loire, the Seine—and I go off to find the blue poster-paint in the art cupboard.

In a little while Miss Millman comes over to my place to check my work and asks me to go to the girl's room and get Frances. Of course, I say, "Yes, Ma'am," even though I am so mad at Frances. What the heck is she doing in the bathroom all this time? I feel I have to keep moving, or I will not have time to finish my map today. But I go off to the girl's room, which is right across the hall and one door down. I push open the heavy swinging door, which is to protect us in case of fire. You should always touch the handle, and, if it's hot, don't open it and go jump out the window instead. I stick my head in and yell crossly, "Frances Mead, you come back to the classroom this minute says Miss Millman, or else," and what do I hear but ol' crybaby Frances start to sob like I had just called her lard ass, which

I didn't, though I heard some mean sixth-grade boys say it to her once. So then I thought maybe she'd fallen and hurt herself because sometimes the floor can be slippery wet in there, so I say, "Are you okay?" She only sobs louder, so finally I go right up to the door and lean against it and whisper, "What's wrong?" She whispers back, "I think I'm dying," and I get out of there fast. I pull open the heavy swinging door and run across the hall, even though we are not allowed to run in the hall. I feel that this emergency situation may warrant breaking a major school rule. I yank open the classroom door and yell, "Miss Millman, you better come to the girl's room and help Frances—she's dying!" Debbie Dexter, who always was a little scene stealer, lets go a shriek as if she's being strangled or something, and she collapses in a dead faint, her white Plaster of Paris hands fluttering down to the floor beside her like two little white doves. Her twin sister, Linda, runs to her side, leans down, and slaps her across the face hard! I could see Linda had probably waited for a long time for the opportunity to do this. Then I remember my mother telling me to concentrate on my assigned work, so I go back to my desk and begin painting black circles to indicate the location of the major cities—Marseilles, Lyons, Calais. Miss Millman is gone a long time. When she finally returns, she has her arm around Frances's shoulders. She takes Frances to the cloakroom and gets her coat and hat, stuffs her into them, and then announces she is taking Frances to the nurse's office, and we should continue working quietly on our projects. I am personally gratified that she does not give Debbie Dexter so much as a glance.

The next day, all the maps are lined up on the counter under the windows. I can see right away that no one else has got as far as I have, which makes me feel good, until I remember poor Frances, who got the least far of anyone due to her battle with leukemia or whatever it is she's dying from. It isn't till weeks later, when all the girls in our class have to go with our mothers after school to the gym to sit with the lights out and watch the scratchy film strip on the reproductive cycle of women, that the nature of Frances's crisis is made clear. On the way home, I ask Mom when all this is going to happen, and she says, "Well, for some girls in your class, it already has." I say, "Really? Like who?" and she says, "Remember Frances Mead in the bathroom? Scared she was dying? The poor thing thought she was bleeding to death because nobody had prepared her."

"Oh," is all I say, but, whew, I am sure glad that this time I wasn't first.

LANI WRIGHT has been an outdoor educator, language teacher, and college administrator. She is currently at work on a book about a pilgrimage journey to Tibet.

CAROL LEM

Creative Writing

He wants to know if his story is any good,
this eighteen-year-old; slightly Asian
like me, a lover of Russian novels.
"Who's the character?" I ask.
"Just somebody I made up," he says,
scratching his head and looking down
at the patched floor of East L.A. College.

He opens a backpack: Dostoyevsky, Turgenev,
Tolstoy topple over his third-person stories.
"Do you ever use the 'I'?"
Again, he fingers his black hair, as though
an answer might be found in the dark roots
where no one sees.
"Don't like to write about myself"

is all he'll give to the small pool of words
filling the next assignment.
I talk about my father who sat in the dark,
the little sounds of the house.
I see him at his desk, a stack of cafe receipts
and orders beside him, as the sweet and sour
smell of a life wafts through the rooms.

I see myself at twenty-two, reading Eliot,
searching for a safe place inside the words
where "I" could wander silent between beginnings
and endings and the man at the Chinese market
who asked, "Don't you speak your own language?"

How could I say my parents don't talk much.
I know only the language of books.

When life at home ended, years later
I would stumble my way back syllable by syllable
and begin those long talks into the night.
By then Mother and Father were gone, but now
they spoke with an ancestral voice.
Who was "i" among the burning incense sticks
and ashes, these borrowed words?

He wants to know if his story is any good.
"Your last name is Gee?"
But I don't speak . . . ," he snaps.
As afternoon light drapes the window,
students file past, each with a story tucked away
in a backpack of other people's stories.
"If you don't tell yours, Eric, somebody else will."

CAROL LEM teaches creative writing and literature at East Los Angeles College. Her poetry has appeared most recently in *Blue Mesa Review, California Quarterly, Cedar Hill Review, Hawaii Pacific Review,* and *Lucid Stone.* Her books include *Don't Ask Why, The Hermit, The Hermit's Journey: Tarot Poems for Meditation,* and *Moe, Remembrance.* Her work is also represented in *What Will Suffice: Contemporary American Poets on the Art of Poetry, The Geography of Home: California's Poetry of Place,* and *Grand Passion, Poets of Los Angeles and Beyond.* Forthcoming books include *Shadow of the Plum* (Cedar Hill Publications) and *Journey to the Interior* (Pennywhistle Press).

ANDREA ROGERS

Scapegoat

COLORLESS AND SILENT, THEY ARRIVE. One by one they pass the security weapon check, follow the sidewalk through the black iron gate, and enter their classrooms.

The school once served the children of Air Force personnel. Then the base was closed, leaving the school empty until the 90s. Now it is used as an alternative high school. Drug abuse, teen pregnancy, loss of family, and just plain bad situations have provided a need for this type of facility.

The students realize they are statistics, but here each one is an individual. Before being admitted, each student is interviewed and must sign a contract making it a definite choice to get an education.

The school year is divided into five sessions or blocks. A block is seven weeks long with two morning classes lasting one hour and fifty

Andrew Wyeth.
Open and Closed.
Watercolor on paper,
$29^3/_4 \times 28^1/_2$ in., 1964.
Private Collection,
©Andrew Wyeth.

minutes each. Students who are able to complete the requirements can graduate in two years.

There are seventy-five people in my first-hour class. "This is Humanities," I tell them. "In here you will learn about literature, art, music, philosophy and religion."

A few know each other and sit together, but the majority stay to themselves, quietly waiting. There are not enough desks. Twelve people balance themselves against the bookshelves along the wall. A couple of boys accidentally knock a shelf of paperbacks to the floor. There is no way they are going to pick them up.

A man stands next to them who looks to be twenty, at least. He is so thin, it is alarming. His hair hangs over his eyes in yellow strands. Acne scars cover his face. He knows he is too old to be here; it shows in his nervous hands, unable to find a place to rest.

The two who knocked down the shelf notice him and begin to laugh. I glare at them, but he seems not to notice. He has had more to endure than ridicule.

I take attendance and promise more desks tomorrow.

Tomorrow there are no more desks. By Friday, I do not need them, five desks sit empty. Class enrollment has "stabilized" at forty-five.

I want to teach them the things that will reconnect them to life, how to be part of humanity, how to overcome failure, but especially, how to be the people they were meant to be.

The majority do not want to learn. They are impossible to teach, interruptions are constant. They do not listen. They are hostile when corrected. They write in books and argue about the work they are assigned to do.

I begin to handle the class differently. I tighten up on discipline, at the same time giving them more work, but breaking up the two hours with an art or writing project related to the material. This is what they need apparently, as it seems to work most of the time. There are still discipline problems, however.

Someone throws a pen, hitting the back of my skirt as I write on the board. The class gasps in unison expecting me to yell at them. I turn to face the students, casually pick up the pen and throw it away. Near the end of class, I am given the name of the one who threw it.

"Robert," Sheila whispers as I pass her desk. I believe her; she has been honest in other things.

But I select the wrong Robert. He is the one nearest the front of the room who screamed obscenities in the face of a teacher's aide, and is one of the first to cause disruptions. For three days, he will sit in in-school suspension. Ironically, I am teaching the concept of "scapegoat."

Two days later, the whisperer, who has been absent, informs me of my mistake. The guilty Robert has been attending class without incident.

"You need to apologize." I tell him in the breezeway between classes. "I know you are the one who threw the pen."

"I didn't mean to hit you with it. I was throwing it at the wastebasket."

This must be the apology. "Next time, walk to the wastebasket, okay?"

He nods.

"Someone else is in trouble because you did not tell the truth. I think he needs an apology from you."

Robert agrees to apologize tomorrow.

The next two days he is absent. When he returns, the other boy is gone.

Today I have assigned *The Titanic*. I tell them to open their books and read silently. Most do. Robert is talking to the student in front of him who is trying to read.

I walk to his desk. He continues to talk. I take his book, close it.

"That's O.K.," he says. "I'm leaving anyway."

"Oh, then why are you here?"

"My dad made me come today, but I'm checking out. I'm going to get my G.E.D."

"Then good luck." I send him to the office to call his father for his ride home.

The next day the other Robert returns. He has completed a response to a quotation, "I can, because I think I can." He tells how he supported himself for a year in an apartment without a job but is vague on the details, explaining that he would be arrested if he included everything.

After class, I talk to him. "I'm sorry that I punished you for something you didn't do. I made a mistake. That happens sometimes with teachers."

He nods, accepting my apology without comment.

Robert did not pass my class the first block of teaching. Shortly after the apology, he quit coming to school, so I was surprised to see him in class the first day of the second block. This time was different. He came almost every day, even though he sometimes slept with his head on his desk. He never disrupted the class as before, and he occasionally shared his opinion during a class discussion. Once or twice he even read aloud.

An administrator asked how he was doing. I showed her the zeros in the grade book but added how much his attitude and behavior had improved. She told me he was holding to his sobriety and going to work regularly.

"That's a lot," I commented, knowing he had no rehabilitation center to help him out.

He didn't make a passing grade the second block either, but then again he is starting a new life. Just because he didn't earn a credit doesn't mean he hasn't learned valuable lessons.

I hope that my apology taught him that we all have room to change. By being treated with respect, he may have gained a small portion of self-respect. I don't know the ending to his story; I just know this time it may be different.

ANDREA ROGERS, a teacher in Scottsdale, Arizona, says that as she wrote about the preceding experience, she tried " to touch on the mystery of teaching: the unknown ending to the daily influence on lives."

ROBERT H. HERZOG

Grades
as Zen Koans

To people who cherish the letter above the spirit, koans appear bewildering, for in their phrasing koans deliberately throw sand into the eyes of the intellect to force us to open our Mind's eye and see the world and everything in it undistorted by our concepts and judgments.

—ROSHI PHILIP KAPLEAU THE THREE PILLARS OF ZEN

FOR MOST OF THE HALF-CENTURY that I've been involved with education, I have battled with grades. When I was a student, grades seemed to a considerable extent arbitrary, and yet they had a powerful influence on my life, including what schools I might get into, what scholarships, if any, I might earn, and even, unfortunately, how I measured my own self-worth.

I suppose I believed that if I were to become a teacher, I would be able to use the system of grades in a more equitable and understandable fashion; at the very least, I would be able to understand the system myself. Quite the contrary. Over thirty years of teaching have shown me that grades lead to confusion more than enlightenment, and probably detract from, rather than accurately measure, learning. However, a series of experiences has led me to understand grades as having a power equivalent to that of a Zen koan. Used in Zen training, a koan is a paradoxical story or riddle, so apparently irrational that it awakens one to a new level of understanding. Perhaps one of the most familiar koans is "What is the sound of one hand clapping?"

Understanding that grades often interfered with the learning they were intended to measure, I saw their kinship to the paradoxes inherent in koans. Perceiving grades as koans, I was awakened to a new understanding of my role as teacher. Often an awakening through the study of koans is as sudden as a splash of water. My awakening through grade koans was more gradual, a series of encounters with students. As I reflect on my experiences with students and grades, it seems my sand-stung eyes are opening to a process that had been operating within me but of which I was, until now, unaware.

PROBABLY THE FIRST TIME I perceived the irrationality associated with grades was with a student who hated my course, and me, until one day he wrote an essay that was clearly an A. After receiving the grade, he made a special trip to my office to tell me how much he loved my course and what a fine teacher I was.

After he left the office, I sat staring out the window. How was I to take this? How could a grade change his evaluation of my instruction so dramatically? His previous visits to my office had been to explain in some detail how deficient were both my teaching methods and my grading. After he received one A, both my teaching and grading had risen immeasurably in his estimation. After years of Zen study, I think I can approach some answers. Grades had the effect of a koan on the young man in that the grades were a barrier that he somehow had to confront and overcome. When he did so, his whole perception of himself changed and thus his world around him with it. I'm not about to suggest that his enlightenment was due to my excellence as a teacher; in fact, my teaching was irrelevant. He must have felt that somehow, mysteriously, he had accomplished something he had thought impossible. Granted, his "enlightenment" was pretty egocentric. But so was my reaction. I didn't recognize then that the grades were a barrier to the relationship of student and teacher and should have been dealt with as such. Neither the student nor I were at a place then where we could be aware of what lay beyond the letter of the grade.

ANOTHER STUDENT who placed a high value on grades took both of us to that higher level of understanding. She was an excellent student, and very grade conscious. Each essay I returned was graded A but not A+. She would come to my office to debate what she felt I had missed. Our conversations were what I'd term friendly bantering. If I'd known Zen at the time, I might have called it a mondo, an exchange of question and answer between a Zen teacher and student, though I probably would have incorrectly identified myself as the teacher. I was unwilling to give her the "plus" because I knew she could raise the level of her work. Perhaps I was as stubborn as she, and I probably was correct in my insistence, though for reasons I was unaware of at the time.

Then occurred what I thought might be a crisis between us. She turned in a paper that was very confusing: unconnected images, tangential references to something obscure. But there was power, mystery, a meaning adumbrated and haunting. A central image of a boy swinging on a church gate, and a funeral, and an empty house. There was so much there, and so much withheld. I didn't grade it, knowing soon she would be at my office, and we would be able to discuss a rewrite. When I handed back the papers, I expected her to stop after class. Nothing. Nor did she stop after the next class, or the next. Finally *I* stopped *her* after one class as she was making her way toward the door. When I asked if she wanted to discuss the paper, she said, "No."

"Are you upset?" I asked.

"No."

"Well," I said smiling. "Why did you complain about every paper except this one that has no grade?"

"With this one," she said, "I don't need a grade. I know it's good; it's exactly what I needed to write, and I'm happy with it, just the way it is."

If I had been familiar with Zen at the time, I would have recognized the close parallels with a Zen student achieving enlightenment, going beyond the lessons, beyond the master, breaking through signs, symbols and letters to the spirit. She had already left me behind.

ANOTHER STUDENT, though she didn't know the word Zen, understood this concept on a deeper level and taught it to me. She was a single mother of four children, each of whom had profound disabilities. Her husband had abandoned her and the children the previous year because he couldn't endure the stress. This forced her to return to school so that she could obtain a job that would enable her to support the family.

She was an attractive, pleasant woman. Her essays were neat but unfocused, for reasons not difficult to understand. Indeed, considering her situation, I marveled she could focus at all, but her papers were, at best, only C papers. She never complained about the grade, nor did she have to tell me how hard she worked on her essays.

Halfway through the course, she showed up for class about twenty minutes after we had started. After class, she apologized for being late, saying she had thought that she had scheduled the tests early enough to make class, but, unfortunately, they had to do some oth-

Lady with a Pomegranate (probably the Goddess Turan). Etruscan bronze, 20.3×8.4 cm. 450–430 BC. Harvard University Art Museums. Arthur M. Sackler Museum. Alpheus Hyatt Purchasing Fund, Francis H. Burr Fund, and through the generosity of 24 Friends of the Fogg Art Museum.

er tests. When I asked if everything was all right, she smiled ruefully and said the tests had confirmed she had a stomach cancer.

She continued the course, never missing or being late for another class, still struggling with her essays, still receiving C grades and never complaining about grades or the life she had been given. John C. H. Wu in *The Golden Age of Zen* states his belief, "That for all the great Zen masters, our whole life is one big koan, which we must break through before we begin to be really alive." My student bore the mystery of her misfortunes as she struggled with grades, patiently and persistently, and with a Buddha-like smile. She did not see the trials as something that interfered with her life; they were her life, and she lived them.

THIS PREPARED ME for what, for now, is the highest point of my awakening to the power of grades as koans. Bob is in his late fifties and suffers from muscular dystrophy. He has great trouble walking and speaking and is, to use the parlance, academically challenged.

I wondered why he was enrolled at a community college; he was retired, so there was no need for a diploma, and academic material was such a struggle for him that it certainly couldn't provide him much pleasure. Why was he taking a course in introduction to literature?

About three-fourths of the way through the course, I called him in to explain to him he needed to withdraw because there was no chance of his passing the course. His hands and face trembled more than usual and tears mixed with the saliva that drooled from his mouth when he spoke. He explained that he had had so many F's and withdrawals that he would lose his financial aid and student status and would not be able to attend classes any more. He said that he loved me and the students in the class, and that coming to this college was all he had to look forward to. Couldn't I find it possible to at least give him a D? He said he would write extra papers. But we both knew, from the many rewrites he had done in the past, they would be a collection of garbled sentence fragments that were little more than a weakly expressed plot summary. I said I'd think it over.

I talked with my friend Derek in the philosophy department. He was a good counselor. He said, "Look at the consequences of each action. If you give him a D or C what will happen? He's not going to transfer anywhere and embarrass you or the college. On the other hand, if you fail him, he'll end up sitting in his room alone, staring at the walls."

In the last class of the semester, as is my custom, I had the students draw their chairs into a circle to give a brief summary of their final papers. When it came to Bob, he said he had no final paper but wanted to thank everyone for being his friend. He had to struggle to get the words out, not only because of his disability, but because of the emotion beneath the words. His face and neck were contorted as his strained voice explained that he knew he hadn't written very good papers and didn't know too much about literature, but he had learned how important friends were. It was difficult to tell if *he* was crying, but most of *us* had tears in our eyes.

It was then I heard the sound of one hand clapping.

But the import of every koan is the same: that the world is one interdependent Whole and that each one of us is that Whole.

KAPLEAU, THE THREE PILLARS OF ZEN

R.H. HERZOG has taught in the English Department at Monroe Community College (Rochester, New York) since 1967. He is currently working on a narrative based on family correspondence and records dating to the mid-nineteenth century.

ELEANORA PATTERSON

Blind Typing

My sister and I took the train
one summer to the city
to typing class
for the Jobs we'd inevitably get.
We had to learn blind typing—
no looking down as
quick brown foxes ran and jumped.
Perfect minds were empty minds,
no encumbrances
to the parade of letters
marching through.

We aimed our fingers precisely.
Firm hits made strong clear letters.
Pinky finger letters, like "A"
were fuzzy
if you landed at all
and didn't get fingers stuck
between keys.

Little bells jingled the end of the line:
the happy carriage rang its readiness
to return.
Strings of speeding letters,
onion skin paper for easy erasure,
test times of wpms
20, 30, 40—faster
until too many mistakes
returned us to 20.

That was the summer we were being prepared
to pass time
exercising precise mindlessness
in the world of work,
in the break between
our supposed-to-lives,
while we waited
for the carriage's return.

ELEANORA PATTERSON learned to type in Philadelphia during the summer
she was sixteen but had no regrets years later when she traded in her manual typewriter, carbon paper, and white-out for a computer. One novel got
lost in the mania of cutting and pasting, but two books for young children
managed their way into print. Even her two years as a secretary, attached to
a dictating machine, had the compensation of fussing over words. Now living in Southern Vermont with her family, writing continues to be an essential companion; in her daytime job, she navigates a quirky patois of English,
Spanish, transmission tech, and marketing.

The Game

"DO YOU PLAY BASEBALL?" I was being interviewed for a teaching job at Parksboro Junior High and the small, thin bespectacled principal was firing questions at me. I thought it odd that he hadn't asked me about my teaching experience. He seemed more interested in my athletic ability. I said that I had been a Little Leaguer in my youth and had played some high school ball. He seemed pleased at that.

"What position are you interested in?" he continued.

"Well, I'd like the seventh-grade English class," I replied. A friend had given me a tip that three teachers were retiring in this district, and their positions were open.

"No, no," the principal said. He chuckled. "I was referring to baseball, actually softball. What position could you play on the faculty softball team?"

"Oh . . . first base, I guess, or the outfield," I said. This was turning into the strangest interview ever.

"I'll tell you why I ask," he said. "At the end of the year we have a student–faculty softball game. Unfortunately, the faculty gets slaughtered every time. The staff has asked me to coach next year, and I have accepted. I figured that while I was interviewing new teachers, I'd keep an eye open for good ballplayers as well."

"I see." At first, I thought that he was kidding, but I nodded and smiled anyway. "So you won't let us down, will you?" he raised one eyebrow in an almost comical way.

"No sir. No, I won't."

"Excellent! You're hired. New staff members will report September first for orientation."

As I drove home I was happy, but perplexed. Had I really landed my first teaching job because I said that I played baseball? It was absurd.

My first teaching year was a real challenge, and I soon learned what did and didn't work in the classroom. Throughout the school year, faculty members would introduce themselves and offer suggestions. At the same time they would manage to squeeze in a question like, "Do you have a good arm?" or "Can you switch hit?" It was all very strange.

Right before Christmas, the physical education teachers threw a big party at their house. Bob and Karen Wesson were married and dedicated to good health. They served fruit and vegetable "cocktails" at their party. One whole room of their house was stuffed with physical fitness equipment. They were both in the peak of health, especially Karen. Every eighth-grade boy and a few male teachers had a serious crush on her. She was blonde, blue-eyed, and extremely well-built. Bob was a massive man with biceps that looked like my leg muscles. At school he was extremely courteous to her—chivalrous would be a better word. He always ran around and opened the car door for her. Whenever she came into the faculty room, he'd jump up and pull a chair out for her. The female teachers would look longingly and sigh—maybe someday they will meet prince charming.

I was reaching into the punch bowl filling my glass with an apple–carrot mixture when Bob approached me.

"My friend owns Bat-A-Rama, and he gives me a great discount. Maybe we could go there some time, and you could sharpen up your batting skills."

"Yeah, thanks, that sounds good. Maybe I will," I said. I knew that he was just dying to see what I could do. Then he'd send his scouting report to my principal and coach, Mr. Casey.

"Great, well let's set it up. How about next Saturday?" he pressed.

"Oh no, next Saturday my friend's getting married," I lied.

"Okay, then the Saturday after that," he said. I could see that he wasn't going to give up.

"No, that's no good," I replied, "I've got to take my car in for a tune-up." I was running out of excuses, but luckily at this point he caught on. He gave me a funny look and shrugged his shoulders. "Suit yourself," he said and strode off.

After that, whenever Bob saw me in the halls he would just grumble and shake his head. He had decided that I was a lost cause. The rest of the year flew by, and suddenly it was June. The day of the student–faculty softball game had finally arrived.

It was a hot, muggy day. The field that formed the back border of the school grounds was dusty and dry. The whole school was there from tiny first-graders to towering eighth-graders. The student team consisted of the best players from the boys' and girls' softball teams. During the regular season, Bob and Karen Wesson coached the very successful teams. Bob's team had won the district championship three years in a row while Karen's girls had gotten to the state championships only to lose by a run. The students were a formidable opponent.

The faculty team was made up of such physical specimens as Bob and Karen, as well as Jack Hurley, a war veteran, and Mr. hanson, the new social studies teacher recruited that year along with myself. The rest of the team consisted of older teachers like Mrs. Laird, the librarian, and the home economics and art teachers. These sweet old ladies were very popular with the students, but possessed only a vague notion of how the game was played. Principal Casey was our coach. He considered himself a student of the game, but was extremely unathletic himself. All through the game he'd yell things like, "They've got the hit-and-run on!" or "Hit the cutoff man!" Poor Mrs. Laird and the others had no idea what he was talking about.

The students opened up the first inning with a vengeance by scoring five runs before we could get an out. Our turn came, and Bob Wesson batting in the cleanup spot walloped a home run with his wife on base to give us our first two runs. I followed Bob as fifth batter and struck out on the first three pitches. I was overanxious and jumped on every pitch regardless of its proximity to the plate. I glanced over at Coach Casey, and he was shaking his head. It seemed silly, but I felt that if I could distinguish myself in this game, I'd be rehired. I didn't want to contemplate the obvious alternative.

The rest of the game slogged along, and each time I batted, I either struck out or hit a towering pop up with my wicked uppercut. It wasn't very encouraging, and meanwhile the students continued to add to their total. Finally, it was our last at bat, and I led off the inning. The score was 11 to 3. We were getting slaughtered again. I remembered what someone had once said about baseball. That it was a wonderful game because it didn't matter how badly you did in the earlier innings. If you could do something spectacular in the last inning, that's what people would remember. With this thought in mind, I approached the plate determined to wait for the right pitch and to swing level. The third pitch was perfect, and I consciously swung down on it, avoiding the vicious uppercut that had ruined my Little League career. I sent a screaming line drive right at the shortstop who instinctively ducked, and the ball skipped into left field. As I ran to first base, I saw my career suddenly get a boost as the left fielder charged the ball, and it took a weird bounce and skidded past her. I streaked to second base and turned toward third. She was still chasing the ball, so I continued to third base. When her throw went awry and missed the cutoff, I ran home and scored our team's fourth run. Our side erupted, and Mrs. Laird congratulated me on my "home run." Of course, any knowledgeable baseball fan would have ruled it an extra base hit with a throwing error, but I thanked her anyway. Mr. Casey seemed pleased in the assurance that he possessed a good eye for talent.

My homer had started a rally. The art and science teacher got hits and poor Mrs. Laird was hit by a pitch to load the bases. The new social studies teacher hit a double that scored two runs and secured his position for the following year. The score was now 11 to 6. The home economics teacher struck out, and our rally started to cool off. We had reached the top of our batting order. The music teacher bunted. This caught the infield off guard, and he landed safely on first, loading the bases again. The next batter was Jack Hurley who was in terrific shape from his army days. He hit a loping single into the outfield, and two more runs crossed the plate. The score was now 11 to 8, and the students began to look worried. The tying run was at the plate. It no longer looked like a massacre. Karen Wesson was next and Bob jumped up, handed her a bat and whispered into her ear. Chivalry was not dead. She had pulled a muscle earlier, and Bob had lovingly massaged it between innings. The female staff melted with envy.

Bob must have said something right. Karen's line drive found a gap in the outfield, and she ended up on third base scoring two more runs. Bob Wesson stood at the plate. A hit would score Karen and tie, but if Bob hit a home run he could win the game. The entire student team stiffened as the outfield fell back to the trees that skirted the edge of school property. Bob took a few practice swings with three bats at once, and then discarded two of them. He stared menacingly at the student pitcher who seemed reluctant to throw the ball.

Bob swung at the very first pitch and sent a shot to deep center. It was a goner, and Karen nonchalantly walked toward the plate as Bob jogged toward first. The staff was exuberant, and some of the infielders started walking off the field. Meanwhile the young center fielder was running toward the line of trees with her glove extended. At the last possible moment she leaped high, and the ball smacked the glove knocking her down. It was a fantastic catch! Bob continued toward second until the young girl held the ball up for all to see. She had not dropped it! Karen went back to third while Bob kicked and clawed at the turf, muttering to himself.

Team spirit deflated like a slashed tire. Karen could've tagged up and tied the game, but everybody thought the ball was gone. Even Coach Casey was at a loss for words. I knew that Karen felt bad, but I felt worse because I was up. As I nervously approached the plate, I realized that the whole school year was boiling down to this one at bat. If I could just get a hit! Then I noticed something. The outfield was still out of position from adjusting to Bob's long-ball threat. There was a huge gap in right center. I knew that I'd have to jump on the first pitch before the outfielders spotted the hole in their defense. I remembered an old trick from my Little League days. As the first pitch approached, I quickly shifted my feet so that they were pointing toward right field. My back was practically to the pitcher. Luckily for me the pitch was outside, and I walloped it right into that gaping hole. Karen scored easily, and the game was tied. I would have gladly settled for a double, but when I reached second, I saw that they were still chasing the ball, so I sprinted to third.

I paused at third base to catch my breath and receive a pat on the back from a colleague. I noticed that both outfielders hesitated when they reached the ball, not sure who should throw it back in. At that moment I had a blinding burst of inspiration, and I took off for home. I realized that if I was out, it would kill the inning, but the game was now tied. If I was safe, however, we would win the game—actually I would win the game. This was definitely a no-lose situation. I saw the throw coming in, and it was going to be close. For a second I debated about sliding, but decided against it. I was never very good at it and besides, I wanted to maintain a little dignity. The throw was dead center, and it almost had me, but it was a bit short. The catcher stepped in front of the plate to catch it and whirled around to tag me. When he did, I lurched sideways, evading him, and crossed the plate with the winning run.

The faculty was ecstatic. Even Mrs. Laird was jumping up and down with delight. The principal was beaming as he walked over to me and shook my hand.

"Congratulations," he said, "I knew I picked a winner the first day I saw you."

"Thank you, Mr. Casey . . . it was nothing." I tried being modest.

"Nothing! Why, this is a first! We've never beaten the students before."

"Well, I'm glad we won," I replied.

"We're going to move you up in the batting order next year."

"Oh . . . uh, thank you." Suddenly, I realized what this meant. I was being rehired after all.

"Don't thank me," he said. "Thank those two home runs of yours."

Throughout the next year, students and faculty alike referred to those two clutch "home runs" in the last inning. I was a bit confused how my hits with errors could be ruled home runs, but I wasn't about to argue the point. In the years that followed, the story of those two "home runs" grew into a legend. My legendary slugging ability afforded me the greatest of honors. Every time I stepped into the batter's box, the outfielders would drop back, the infield would play deep, and the pitcher would flinch when she delivered the ball. It took another ten years before we could beat the students again, but it didn't matter. I was still treated as a deadly threat when I came to the plate. Principal Casey was equally convinced because he kept moving me up in the batting order every few years.

After many years of teaching, I am proud to say that I have helped to budge that great Sisyphean stone of pedagogy a bit. But what I am proudest of is that I am now the lead-off batter for the faculty softball team. Sadly, dear old Mrs. Laird retired this year and left a vacancy. There's exciting news, however, about a young woman who pitched her college softball team right into the state championships. It's rumored that not only did she major in library science, she's also a spectacular long-ball hitter. Not a day goes by that we don't pester Mr. Casey to get her in for an interview.

JOHN A. CONROY has been teaching for twenty-six years at Gibbsboro Elementary School in New Jersey. His hobbies include chess, oil painting, ham radio, and creative writing.

PART IV

Mentoring

Mountain Men

Oh Minute Men and Paul Revere
And foreign fellows too:
Cortez, Cornwallis, Lafayette
Who sailed the angry sea
In little ships with little meat.
They kept their muskets clean and neat
For victory or for defeat.
But that is History now.

And most I like the Mountain Men,
A grisly greasy crew.
John Colter and Jim Bridger
They wintered in the snow,
All on their own and all alone,
Except at Rendezvous.

They saw the first of mountains,
The eagle and the bear,
The strange and salty fountains,
The swift and changing hare.

To stand upon the edge of things
Without companions by,
To have a cap of beaver,
To hear the coyote cry,
To carve initials in a stone,
To think you did it all alone,
Now *that's* the thing for me.

—JULIA RANDALL

TERRY MAROTTA

The Tender Intent

Lynn Chadwick.
Winged Figure.
Bronze with green
and brown patina,
17¼×21×7 in.
Portland Museum of Art,
Maine. Lent by Mildred
Otten, The Albert Otten
Collection, 10.1993.9.

"I'M GETTING A NOSE RING," our fifteen-year-old announced, perching on our front porch railing with the thoughtless easy balance of the young.

"Uh, I don't think you want to do that, Carrie," my husband said gently but with a certain definite quality.

How quickly we get drawn into power struggles with the young, was all I could think then, overhearing this exchange from my spot just inside the house. From the time they are tiny, kids yearn to make their own decisions, and in their own time, as any parent surely knows who has struggled with toilet-training's occasional victories and sudden soggy reversals.

Adolescents especially seem sure their parents live only to control them. Perhaps their real maturity begins when they realize that in truth we wish just the opposite; that in fact we yearn for that day when they come to control themselves and with poise and discernment hold dominion over the oft-conflicting impulses all humans struggle to reconcile.

But did Carrie know her dad wished this for her? I walked outside to join them and realized I couldn't say, even as I listened to their conversation. It was her father talking now. "It's a mistake. It's a bad decision, doing something like that to your body."

She responded in her usual way, which was to pause, look at him with genuine love, then speak in the sweet voice of reason. "Well maybe it is and maybe it isn't. But Dad, you must know it's nothing compared to some of the other decisions I'm making about my body."

And the truth of that remark gave us both pause. Because of course she was right. On every weekend, in every after-school hour, on whatever other occasions she may be away from adult eyes and in the company of peers, she was certainly deciding things: whether to accept the proffered beer or say no; whether to experiment with drugs or to walk away; whether to become sexual with a boyfriend or to wait.

"Some decisions only the individual can make," is what she was telling us in all but words. "I want to be the one to decide," she meant. "It's true autonomy that I yearn for now," she seemed to be saying.

And I guess in a way, we had encouraged this yearning. Hadn't we always, all through her little-girl years, let her have at least some choice in the daily decisions? The bath now, or after supper? The nap first, and then the Playdough pie crust after, or vice versa?

Additionally, I couldn't forget the fact that since she was an infant, she had spent one whole day a week in the presence of my own mom, also named Caroline but called Cal instead of Carrie, as strong and independent a woman as ever lived, who in the last stage of her life came to live in a retirement community near me and began immediately radicalizing the other residents. ("Those years we kept house and minded children!" she would boom good-naturedly to her pals, tiny ancient ladies clinging to canes and walkers. "People, we should have been earning *Social Security!*")

Once, when she was a more youthful seventy-five, we'd spent the day at Mom's house, concluding with a big family dinner, at the end of which Carrie, then four-and-a-half, expressed a desire for seconds of ice cream.

"Ah no," we many grownups murmured, shaking our sagacious heads. "Afraid not." "You've had enough," we cooed like so many pigeons.

She paused a minute, then said in the measured way that was her way even then, "I can't reach the freezer and get more. If I were taller, I'd just go get some."

I don't think any other child of ours ever spoke up at such a young age to invoke what she saw as a principle of fairness. It was certainly the first time David and I were invited to consider some things about the power a person can hold over others, and the slow seductive way one grows accustomed to wielding it. Our eyes met over the table; then one of us jumped up and scooped her some ice cream.

And now, of course, she *was* taller and seemed to be sensing in her fresh growth that many of the old strictures might no longer feel right and that some circumstances in which she found herself now called for changing.

The school she attended, for example, was beginning to feel on some level uncongenial to her. I remember we had been riding in the car together, just a week before the nose-ring announcement, when she first tried putting words around it.

"I think I need to change schools," is how she'd broached the subject in the penultimate month of sophomore year.

I asked why.

"I don't know. It's a lot of things. For one thing, I think I should have to work harder to get grades as good as I get. But mostly . . ." she paused here a moment, then went on, slightly abashed. "Mostly I feel in a strange way lonely—as if I haven't yet found my true friends."

We know she was shyer—more reticent—than most of the kids she spent time with, a quality I attributed to the fact that since age seven she had been the patient victim of brain-shattering migraine-pain, which marked her early with a definite caution. I still remember the sixth-grade spring when her Girl Scout troop began excitedly planning a weekend trip to New York City. Eleven-year-old Carrie announced that she wouldn't be going. "I could never do a thing like that," she had quietly told us. "You know I'd only get a headache—and *then* what would they do with me?"

But I had noticed that just lately, about six months before, she had begun growing bolder; had set down her ever-present book and gone out to meet the world some.

And people took to her. Both in school and on the sidewalks at the big city we live near, she was kind to the odd and lonely. If she had money, she gave some to all the lost and unlucky who asked for it. If she didn't have money, she always stopped a moment and stood chatting, instead of hurrying past, as so many of us do. Seeing her do this taught us another lesson that involved moving more slowly and compassionately through one's day. It was a lesson her busy parents did well to heed too, in these hectic middle years of life.

So she'd begun sensing that she was different: both from her old self and from the mainstream, too. And maybe she just wanted some outward sign of this difference.

In this case, she got her nose ring—or to speak more accurately, had a tiny hole bored by her best friend's surgeon–dad in the delicate flange of one nostril, in which she set a tiny diamond stud—and began her eleventh-grade year at a new school, where the homework was hard and the classes small, and the teachers strict, savvy, and loving all at once. She studied hard all day and every weekend. Senior year, she bought a used car and talked the school into giving her sports credit for the effort of driving all alone, an hour-and-a-half each day, to get to a rowing club where she began mastering the daunting skills of Crew.

Later, in college, she studied hard as well. She rowed there too, and played, ran four or five miles a day because she noticed that intense bursts of exercise every day kept away migraines; and one summer did an intense internship that involved sitting all day in high Colorado meadows counting hummingbird hits on a particular kind of flower growing by those mountain roadways. She stepped up her commitment to the environment and even began fishing cans and bottles out of other people's wastebaskets to bring home and recycle properly.

But when she told us at twenty that she meant to have a chain motif tattooed in an inch-wide band clear around one bicep, we felt for a moment as though she were fifteen again.

And once again it was her father who spoke first. "You know if you do that, you might never get a job in the business world."

"Dad!" she said as if happy to be the bearer of such wonderful tidings, "I don't want a job in business. It's the Secretary of the Interior's job I have my eye on!"

She was poised and competent and just coming into her powers. Was this still the old struggle for autonomy, the old need to assert herself freshly?

It wasn't at all, as I learned later that evening when I came upon her, studying some object closely and rendering it in pen and ink on her sketch pad. Drawing closer, I could see she had in one hand the unusual wedding ring of that same Grandma Cal whose passing some few years back changed us all when, in our living room, at her own eightieth-birthday celebration, she closed her eyes and died before the eyes of forty horrified family members. It was that simple. The color drained from her face and her heart stopped. The ambulance came and took us to the hospital, and an hour later I was home again, clutching her evening purse and her large-faced watch and lovely ring, with its near-inch-wide band delicately carved in leaves and flowers.

She had worn it every day, decades past the time her brief and tragic marriage ended. I never saw her without it. On the day she died, I put it on; wore it for a solid year and on selected days since then. I wore it when I needed her strength. I wore it so that, looking quickly at my own hands, I could pretend that they were hers.

Carrie knew I still needed my mom's ring. She would never ask to take it from me. So she was planning to have the design of its lovely intertwining leaves and flowers inked in a delicate chain on her own person, where she would carry it always. Perhaps realizing that this tender intent was what lay behind our daughter's latest enterprise marked another step in our education as parents.

Well, Carrie's childhood is over now. As if to mark its closing, she took the first semester of her senior year off from Wellesley. "I want to go by myself and see some things," she told us. "I want to live in the desert a while, and then maybe, the Arctic Circle."

She did just that. With her delicate jaw narrow as a collie's and her eyes both green and brown marbled together and her grandmother's totem inked in the skin and circling one perfect bicep, she went to Arizona and for two months delivered people their morning papers at 4 AM in the loneliness of the desert. She drove north and north some more, deep into Alaska, and yes, clear to the Arctic Circle, from which she sent us a postcard saying the ice was the color of antifreeze.

And later, with the semester drawing to a close, six days before she was due home for Christmas, she started driving back. She told us afterward that on the day she turned her car east, she took out a piece of verse by T.S. Eliot that she had long kept in the glove compartment and taped it to her dashboard. They are a famous four lines of verse that seemed to explain to her, and to us on hearing them, the purpose of her journey. "We shall not cease from exploration," they begin, "And the end of all our exploring will be to arrive where we started, and know the place for the first time."

Is the journey home always the longest journey? I think it might be, by the same strange logic by which it is true that the goal of all education is not a layering on but a peeling away, to reveal and bring forth the shining self every person started with in childhood.

It has been a privilege for David and me to have brought several young people along toward adulthood, not just the three born to us but the three or four or five who have come by other means to shelter in our family, and if we are sure of anything, we are sure of this: young people do yearn desperately to stand on their own feet and announce themselves to the world; but they yearn even more to spend themselves in love and in many deeds of courage and valor. They know that our purpose here is a high purpose. We adults know this too; only sometimes we forget and need them to remind us.

TERRY MAROTTA is an author, syndicated columnist, and radio commentator living in Winchester, Massachusetts.

THOMAS R. SMITH

The Game

He barely gives the morning-shadowed street a glance,
crosses, small and alone, in the fragrance of lilacs.
He knows the way to school, wears a tiny backpack,
his cropped hair whitening with sun as he skips,
head bobbing, eyes upward and open to all flowering.
On the sun-lit sidewalk he walks, lingering;
when he comes to a patch of shade, he runs; arrives
at another bar of sunlight, walks. The strength
in him boundless, hc advances the future, hurtling
or lolling, though he still lives mostly for play,
it being equally gorgeous to fling himself headlong
in the coolly ecstatic tunnels of lilacs or to loiter
in the sunnier precincts of this game he has invented
himself at the beginning of the world, in May.

Opposite:
Kate Ransohoff.
Illustration for
"The Black Pearl"
that appeared in the
Chrysalis Reader:
Power of Play (1996).

THOMAS R. SMITH is a poet living on the banks of the Kinnickinnic River in River Falls, Wisconsin. His most recent book of poems is *The Dark Indigo Current* (Holy Cow! Press, 2000). He teaches poetry classes at The Loft in Minneapolis.

Milton Hebald.
Harvest.
Bronze sculpture, 1959.
66 in. height.
The University of Arizona
Museum of Art, Tucson.
Gallagher Collection.

Learning a New Language

"UP THE HILL WE GO," I said to one-year-old Sally. I held her hand as we approached a steep rise that led to Cortland Hill Orchards. "Uppy, uppy, uppy," she repeated as she walked slowly up the hill on her sturdy legs.

It was one of those magnificent fall days with brilliant reds, yellows, and oranges painted among the maples, contrasting with the rich blue sky. I smiled to myself. It had become a tradition—to bring my group of preschoolers to this apple orchard in the fall, to pick apples, to enjoy autumn's bounty. We planned to join another family child-care group on this trip. They were waiting for us in the orchard.

Some of my older children called to one another as they darted up the hill toward the orchard. I walked with Sally behind Isaac, seven years old, as his stiff, unbalanced gait was supported by his aide, Linda—my children call her Isaac's helper.

"Let's open the gate, Sal."

"Me open, me open," Sally loudly pronounced as I picked her up to reach its handle. I turned to Isaac and asked him to help push the gate open. He lifted his arm, keeping his hands in their typically curled-in position, and pushed the gate open with Sally. Then he turned to Sal and smiled, making happy sounds.

Isaac joined my group this year. I have managed an early childhood program in my home for sixteen years. My group of six children range in age from one-and-a-half to seven-year-olds. The foundation of my work with children is to help them learn to be accepting, caring, and loving with one another. During previous years, I have worked with children with challenging behavior and emotional issues. So, when I agreed to enroll a seven-year-old with multiple disabilities (as part of his home schooling), I welcomed the opportunity to learn how to integrate a child with special needs that were new to me.

"Come on, Laura!" shouted four-year-old Ashley. "Wow! Look at those *huge* apples," she called back to us as she ran underneath one of the abundantly full apple trees, gathering apples quickly and dropping them into her basket.

Coming to this orchard with young children is like a fairyland for me. Set on top of a grassy hill, surrounded by a tall wooden fence to keep the deer out, the trees have low-growing branches that even toddlers can reach. This was a field trip that included all ages and abilities.

Sally held my hand tightly as we approached Elly's family child-care group. I could tell Sally was not sure about seeing some faces she did not recognize. Isaac walked ahead of us, swinging his head to watch three-year-olds Patty and Maggie as they passed him. They had recognized friends in Elly's group. Isaac really likes Patty and Maggie, particularly Patty. I have wondered, is it her vivacious energy, her curly hair, her loud voice? Typically, Patty does not slow down to give attention to Isaac.

Patty and Maggie yelled to their friend, four-year-old Allie, who was sitting on the grass next to Elly eating an apple. Isaac, his helper, and I continued walking slowly into the orchard. Allie and I met eyes. "Hi, Allie. Do you remember me? I saw you when we were on a hayride together a few weeks ago. Do you remember?" Allie smiled at me. Before he could reply, I saw his face change as he noticed Isaac walking stiffly toward him, partially supported by his helper. I could see Allie's face take on a quizzical, confused look. I imagined he was thinking: Why does he walk like that? What's wrong with him? Is he sick? Will he get better? Will he hurt me? I'm not sure I want him near me.

I sat down beside Allie.

"This is Isaac. His body doesn't work the same way that yours does. He needs help to walk and to use his body. Let me introduce you."

I looked at Sally. She had placed her little hand purposefully onto Isaac's arm and was "helping" him sit down. I spoke to Isaac.

"Why don't you sit down so we can meet Allie, Patty's friend."

And then it happened, like returning to a well-known childhood place as an adult and a perceptual change becomes apparent. I realized, by seeing Isaac through Allie's eyes, that I had changed since first meeting Isaac five months previously. When I look at Isaac now, I don't first see a seven-year-old boy with disabilities. My awareness of his disabilities frames the picture, but at the focal point is a child who loves music, the sounds and rhythm of language, and being with his peers. He loves his peers. When I first met Isaac during the previous summer, I was sitting with his mother, discussing his disabilities and the prospect of enrolling him in my program. I was excited about gaining new knowledge, but apprehensive. Could I really do it? Isaac then knee-walked into the kitchen. This was his mode of moving from place to place. I was startled. I saw a child, obviously older than a kindergartner, yet moving stiffly and making sounds I couldn't understand. Could I help the children in my group become accepting and caring of Isaac? Could I help Isaac feel safe and secure in my program? I wasn't sure. But I knew I needed to try.

Allie seemed to relax. He turned and called out to Patty, "Let's go fill our baskets with apples!" Allie ran off with his basket to join Patty under an apple tree.

Four-year-old Megan came over and asked if I could help her pick some apples she had spied on a high branch nearby. I agreed, asking her if she'd walk with Isaac and me, and would she carry his basket with him. Megan consented. Isaac's helper went off with Sally toward a group of children gathering apples from the ground under a tree. As we walked, I couldn't help but think of how far we had come since early September, in terms of including Isaac in our group.

It was clear to me that my children had "gotten used to" Isaac; they were growing fond of him. I could think of many examples of how the children help Isaac during our day together. In the playroom, Ashley helps Isaac put " little people" into their basket. One-year-old Uriah plays the piano with Isaac. Three-year-old Josh acts out being frogs with Isaac during circle time. Four-year-old Megan pulls Isaac's chair out for him at snack time. But I continue thinking we need to reach another level. We need to learn Isaac's language. If we can find ways to enter his world, perhaps he can enter our own fast-moving, fast-talking world. I believe the key is to have conversations with Isaac. This may in turn lead to a give-and-take occurring between Isaac and the other children. This naturally occurs among "typically developing" children in their play.

Isaac turned his head toward the red apples hanging heavily on the branches. I put my hand on top of his, and together we picked an apple. Isaac and I are building a store of memories of doing things together. It is not uncommon for me to "change places" with Isaac's helper. Megan held the basket under the apple, and Isaac clumsily dropped the apple in. Sally called out from under the tree, "Appa. Appa. SalSal appa." Sally was biting into a giant apple. Isaac turned toward another apple, looking ready to pick it and drop it into the basket. He heard Patty and jerked his head toward her. She was picking an apple from a tree behind him. Isaac called out to Patty. It sounded like he was saying, "Great!" Patty answered back, "Look at all my apples, Isaac!"

Our baskets were full. Elly and I called the children together. We held hands in a circle. It had been a lovely visit to the orchard. Our closing circle was a dance we have done together many times. Isaac was helped by his aide to hold hands with Patty on one side and Megan on the other. Together our group of twelve children and several adults chanted as we moved in a circle:

Gallop my pony.

Gallop on.

Hey de ho the Summer's gone.

We're riding into Autumn now.

The leaves are falling from the bough.

So, stop! My pony, Whoa!

The children giggled, Isaac smiled, and I knew that we were riding together into a new season.

LAURA LAWSON TUCKER, M.Ed., is an early-childhood educator in Guilford, Vermont. She has worked and played with young children and the teachers of young children for many years. She welcomes her new journey to learn about including all children and their families in early-childhood programs.

DAVID D. JONES

Why My Grandfather Didn't Play for the New York Yankees

I WAS JUST A SKINNY KID BACK IN 1962, small for my age, too, so the coach put me at second base where Little League coaches always seem to put the littlest kids on the team, especially those who wear thick glasses and can't play well, which pretty much summed me up in those days. Despite my deficiencies at the sport, I made up my nine-year-old mind that I wanted to be a good baseball player. My love for the game was matched only by my love for chocolate ice cream, which my mother bought for me at McGuire's Ice Cream Parlor in Glenside, the small town north of Philadelphia where I grew up.

What I enjoyed most during the summer was watching the Phils on television while consuming gobs of ice cream. (No matter how much I ate, I never gained any weight—I wish I could say the same now.) I never went to the games because my father, an accountant for a manufacturing firm, detested baseball with the same fervor that characterized my love for the sport. When I told him I wanted to play Little League, the most he could manage was a grunt over the financial section of the *Philadelphia Inquirer*. He never mentioned my participation in the national pastime, and he never came to see me play. He considered baseball frivolous, maybe because he had to quit school when he was sixteen to work in a shirt factory to help support his family after his father died. My mother had no interest in baseball, either; her face went blank when I brought up the subject.

When my grandfather came to live with us, I found someone in the family who loved baseball just as much as I did. My mother's father, Theodore T. Smith, who everyone called Ted—even me because he asked me to—was eighty-two years old. A widower, he had been an insurance salesman before his health began to fail, which is why he came to live with us. I think he knew even then that he had only a few years to live.

Ted was a tall, slender man who walked with a cane. Despite his ill health, he wore a perpetual half-smile and radiated an inner peace. After I grew up, I thought of him as a kind of skinny Buddha. He didn't talk much, but I always felt calmer and more accepting of myself in his presence. He was as thrilled as I was when I announced over dinner one night that I had made Little League. I didn't mention that everyone who tried out had made the team because only eight other kids showed up.

Ted beamed and said, "Bobby, that's wonderful."

Predictably, my mother's concern was for my safety. "Don't hurt yourself," she admonished.

My father grunted into his asparagus and changed the subject. Right from the start things didn't go well in Little League . I could catch the ball pretty well, but I was barely able to reach first base after fielding a ground ball. My most serious problems were at the plate. No matter how hard I swung at the ball in a game, which was as hard as I could, the most I could manage was to hit dribblers to the infielders, which infuriated me because in batting practice I often hit the ball pretty far, considering my size. My worst fault was that I always struck out with the bases loaded, which didn't endear me to the coach or my teammates. When I stepped to the plate with the sacks jammed, a collective moan would arise from our bench, and when I struck out, which was as inevitable as death and taxes, the coach would shake his head as if to say how could he be expected to win with me on the team. I just didn't have it in the clutch. My problem was panic. When a game became tense, my mouth filled with cotton, my stomach turned queasy, and my knees shook.

As if these drawbacks weren't enough, I also had an attitude problem. I had an aversion to advice, maybe because my father and I didn't see eye-to-eye. I had the same antipathy to helpful suggestions as cats have to taking a bath. Whatever the coach said to me, and he said plenty, went in one ear and out the other.

As the season wore on, it turned out that we had an excellent team, which was good or bad depending on how you looked at it. The other kids were better than I was, which helped our won-loss record, but I looked bad by comparison, and by the end of the season they were teasing me for striking out so much. They called me "Four Eyes," a name I loathed.

Ted came to every Little League game, maybe because he didn't have anything better to do, being in poor health and all, but I like to think it was because he loved me. He never said anything when I made an out, but when I got a hit he would holler, "'Atta boy, Bobby," or "Good going, Bobby," or "Give 'em hell, Bobby."

Afterwards, win or lose, he would take me to McGuire's Ice Cream Parlor and treat me to chocolate ice cream, and we would talk about the game. Ted liked to second guess the coach. He would say stuff like, "I would have walked Evans to get to Miller," or "I wouldn't play Johnson in the outfield. I'd put him at first base," or "I'd have put in a relief pitcher sooner."

With three games left, our team, the Tigers, was two games behind our arch rivals, the much-maligned Dragons, who were known to be poor sports. The Dragons had completed all their games except for their final game with us. For us to play them for the league championship, we had to win two preceding games with a lesser team. In those two must-win games, I struck out three times with the bases loaded, went zero for twenty, and made six throwing errors. I played so badly my teammates stopped speaking to me, and the coach looked the other way when he saw me coming. Despite my performance, the Tigers won both games, 19 to 18 and 17 to 16. The final game approached with us locked in a tie with the Dragons for first place.

After our 17 to 16 win, Ted took me to McGuire's Ice Cream Parlor. I was having my usual, chocolate ice cream, and Ted was having his usual, a cup of hot tea (he drank tea hot, even in the summer), when I announced I was quitting Little League.

"Quitting never solved anything," Ted said with a frown. I pushed my chocolate ice cream to one side. "I stink," I said, tears rolling down my cheeks.

"Now, Bobby," Ted said, worry creasing his brow.

As I sat there wallowing in self-pity and self-loathing, the season came into glaring perspective: the taunts of my teammates, the coach's discouraged glances, my failure to hit the ball out of the infield, my inability to come through in the clutch, all epitomized by my inevitable whiffing with the sacks full.

"I'll never be good at baseball," I moaned.

"Sure you will," Ted said, patting my hand reassuringly.

But my mind was made up and there wasn't anything Ted could say or do that would change it. "I'll never play baseball again," I said with finality.

Ted seemed lost in thought. Then he leaned in my direction and said in a confidential manner, "Bobby, did I ever tell you why I didn't play for the New York Yankees?"

My jaw dropped open. "You were a baseball player?"

"That's right."

"And you almost played for the New York Yankees?"

"Do you want to hear about it?"

"Yea," I said eagerly, putting my misery on hold.

He took a sip of tea and began. "I loved baseball when I was your age. There wasn't a Little League then, of course. My friends and I had to play in empty fields and parking lots. We used rocks for bases and foul lines. I played every chance I could because, like you, I wanted to be good at the game.

"When I wasn't playing ball with my friends, I'd practice by throwing pebbles in the air and hitting them with the sawed off handle of a broomstick. That sharpened my hitting eye."

"Wow!" I said. I had never thought of that.

"By the time I was eighteen, I was considered the best hitter in the whole county. Some compared me to Shoeless Joe Jackson."

"To Shoeless Joe?" I said, my eyes filled with wonder. I had read almost all there was to read about baseball's legendary heroes.

"That's right," he said with a smile. "A scout approached me one day. He asked me if I wanted to try out for the New York Yankees. This was in 1927 when Babe Ruth and Lou Gehrig were playing for the Bronx Bombers. The Yankee manager, Miller Huggins, invited me to spring training."

"Holy cow!" I said, hardly able to contain myself.

"Huggins was excited about me because in the batting cage I'd hit every pitch a country mile. I was so good in practice that the Sultan of Swat himself, Babe Ruth, quit jawing with his teammates one afternoon and came over to watch me hit. He just stood there shaking his head in admiration and awe.

"That first week of spring training, Huggins took me aside and said if I could hit half as well in a game as I could in practice, he'd make me part of Murderer's Row, which was, if you know your base-ball, Babe Ruth, Lou Gehrig, Bob Meusel, and Tony Lazzari."

It might seem incredible that I believed the story, but you must remember that this was the same nine-year-old boy who believed in Santa Claus and the Easter Bunny.

"What happened then?" I asked.

Ted shook his head and stared sadly into space. When he spoke, his words were tinged with sorrow and remorse. "I could hit the ball a ton in practice, but I didn't do well in any of the games with other teams. I seldom hit the ball out of the infield, and I always struck out with the bases loaded."

Ted paused for effect, then said, "Bobby, I played so badly I was cut from the team."

"Really?" I said with a mixture of sadness and relief.

I felt sad that Ted hadn't made the Yankees, but I also felt relieved because now I had an excuse for my defects at the plate. Striking out with the bases loaded was apparently a family trait. I could hardly blame myself for a genetic flaw.

"I didn't realize until years later what I'd done wrong," Ted went on.

"What?" I said, all ears.

"I was trying too hard. I forgot that baseball is a game and that the main reason I was playing was for the fun of it. I swung too hard, which is why I struck out so often. You have the same problem, Bobby. Here's my advice. First, relax when you step to the plate. Then watch the ball all the way from the mound until you actually hit it. And don't swing with all your might. Just try to meet the ball. You'll do best by swinging moderately hard with your weight moving for-ward."

"Okay," I said, enthused again about baseball.

That evening I asked my mother for a broom I knew she wasn't using any more and asked my father to saw off the handle. I spent the next several days in the backyard hitting pebbles with my broom-stick. It took a lot of concentration because the broomstick was nar-row, and the stones were small.

During the championship game with the Dragons, I came up in the second inning with the bases loaded and the score tied, 7 to 7. I ignored the collective groans of my teammates. As usual, my mouth turned to cotton and my stomach did flip-flops, but I had enough presence of mind to take Ted's advice. I kept my eye on the ball and swung only moderately hard at the first pitch while shifting my weight forward.

There was a loud crack as bat met ball. The baseball sailed high and deep into left center field. I was off like a shot, running at full speed as the left and center fielders converged on the ball. It fell between them and rolled all the way to the fence. Both had been play-ing in because of my size and had to run a long way to reach the ball.

I didn't stop running until I crossed home plate. My teammates were so surprised they didn't even congratulate me. They just sat on the bench and stared at me in disbelief. Even the coach looked stunned. My crowning moment, though, came in the last inning. The Dragons scored five runs in the top of the inning to go ahead, 14 to 13. Things looked bleak. I came to bat in our half of the inning with two outs and the bases loaded. I knew if I didn't come through, we'd lose the championship.

I stepped into the batter's box, took a deep breath, and waited for a good pitch. When I got one, I took Ted's advice again. I swung mod-erately hard, shifted my weight forward, and just tried to meet the ball. I connected and watched with glee as the ball flew over the pitch-er's head and into center field for a base hit.

The center fielder, who had been playing deep because of the home run I'd hit earlier, had to run in to get the ball. By that time, the runners on second base and third base had scored and we had won the game and the championship. My teammates got over their amazement at my new prowess, rushed over, picked me up, and car-ried me from the field on their shoulders. Ted gave me a big hug af-ter the game. It was a day I'll never forget.

Looking back on it, I'm sure Ted knew I wouldn't have taken his advice if he had just come out with it. The salesman in him found a way to get through to me, and from that day on I've never been averse to taking advice from anyone (even though my father and I still don't see eye-to-eye on most things).

My baseball career ended with Little League. When I grew up, I became an accountant like my father. Ted died a year after my mo-ment of glory, and I really missed him. I didn't realize until after his death that he'd made up the whole story. By subtracting his age when he died from the current year, I was left with the undeniable fact that he was forty-seven in 1927, much too old for him to have tried out for the Bronx Bombers. By that time, though, the lesson he taught me had been learned. Today, when I'm tempted to try too hard, I think of what he told me so long ago, smile to myself, and then con-centrate on the task at hand and just do my best without pressing too hard. It has always worked.

DAVID D. JONES's short stories and feature articles have appeared in *American Astrology, Dogwood Tales, Horoscope,* and various other periodi-cals, including the Chrysalis Reader.

MARJORIE ANDERSON

Alan's Choice

TODAY ALAN SAYS, "THE REASON GOD TOOK AWAY HALF OF ME is because he built the other half so perfect." Conceit or humility? I call it coping.

It was the night of high school graduation, and Alan had just completed his junior year at the rural Oklahoma school where I teach. "There goes trouble," I said to my husband as he pulled into the filling station beside us.

Alan was not a troublemaker, but the pickup seemed enormous, and he seemed very small behind the wheel. Still, he could have been any other teenager anticipating the evening's activities.

My observation was ominous in the light of what was to come. After that night's commencement, Alan and three friends drove to a dirt road north of town to "jump the bumps"—a foolish but not uncommon pastime here. No alcohol or drugs were involved, just high spirits.

On a final jump, Alan lost control of the vehicle. It rolled into a wheat field and burst into flames. The others were thrown clear. Alan was trapped beneath the burning pickup, his spine severely damaged and his entire body critically burned.

Alan had been at the Baptist Burn Center in Oklahoma City four months when the next school term began. Though bedridden, he was determined to graduate with his friends in the spring. With help, he could earn first semester credits and possibly return to the classroom after Christmas. I agreed to be his tutor.

The first time I saw Alan at the burn center I very nearly fainted. In the waiting room, his mother had tried to steel me for the shock. So had the nurses who helped me into the white smock and showed me where to wash my hands. Their words could not prepare me for the stranger lying in that bed. The smile was the same. Everything else had changed.

Alan's right arm was a stub, and all but two fingers on his left hand were gone. Only patches of that beautiful curly hair remained. One ear was mutilated, and he was horribly scarred over most of his face and body. The damage to his spine made it doubtful he would ever walk again.

It was all I could do to maintain self-control. Alan immediately took charge. He called my attention to what the plastic surgeon had already done for him. He was enthusiastic about surgeries yet to come.

From the beginning, Alan made it clear he intended to win . . . and that he would be in control of how he did it. That very day he insisted on beginning a rigorous program that included English literature and upper level history and psychology.

I began my teaching duties full of sympathy for the victim of a disfiguring fire. My sympathy quickly turned to respect, for Alan was eager to learn and a delight to teach.

I made the trip to Oklahoma City twice a week for a month. The nurse gave us a white sheet to use as a screen for the overhead projector. The minute I walked into his hospital room and began taping the sheet to the wall, he dismissed his family, friends, and nurses. He was in school now, and not to be disturbed.

As I taught, I also learned. During breaks, Alan spoke of his plans for the future, and of his family and friends. One of his friends in particular, Tom, had given me no end of trouble the previous year.

Alan pled Tom's case so well that I came to want to know him better. Because of the different perspective Alan gave me, I learned to appreciate Tom and other mischievous but good-hearted students like him.

When Alan was well enough to handle a wheelchair, he came home, which was only an hour's drive from the burn center where he would undergo therapy and additional surgery. He convalesced under his mother's care.

I had misgivings when I learned of the impending transfer. Only his most supportive friends had seen him since the accident; the others might be cruel. The burn suit and mask he wore to cut down on scarring concealed most of the damage, but it accented his differentness. I wanted to protect him from stares and ridicule and . . . I don't know, from life-ever-after, I guess.

On the day he came home, I was helping students decorate the cafeteria for homecoming. Alan's mother rolled his wheelchair into the midst of maybe a hundred rambunctious teenagers. Immediately, you could hear a pin drop.

In no time, Alan was surrounded by the finest young people in the universe. No one cried. No one fainted. Certainly, no one laughed. I began to breathe again.

Alan wore the same smile and exhibited the same help-them-through-it attitude he had shown me that first day in the hospital.

Three of his buddies, including Tom, of course, hauled him carefully out of his wheelchair and supported him while his mother took a group picture. Then it was back to business for everyone but me. I had to get out of there before I embarrassed myself.

The next week, we set up school in the living room of his home. Alan sat in a stuffed chair, his feet on a hassock. I sat on the floor beside the overhead projector and flashed his lesson onto the blank TV screen.

One by one, Alan overcame obstacles in the way of his success. Before the accident he had been right-handed. That arm was gone now. A little rubber grip with a pencil attached to it was strapped onto the two remaining fingers of his left hand. It wasn't long before he learned to write quite legibly.

One Sunday afternoon I went to Alan's house for our regular session and was treated to something far from regular. I came in the back way through the sliding glass doors and saw Alan across the room in the stuffed chair, grinning. His mother said to wait at the door, that Alan had something to show me.

As I watched in amazement, he pulled himself up out of the chair and took two steps toward me. As his mom and dad helped him back to his chair, I felt someone needed to help me. Alan wasn't supposed to ever walk again.

Could it be a miracle? No, I assured myself. Something that wasn't expected to grow back together did grow back together. I couldn't help thinking his smile had helped. Who knows? I finally conceded. Maybe it was a miracle.

After Christmas Alan came back into the regular school system. He started the second semester in a wheelchair, but it wasn't long before he was on his own two wobbly legs.

I shuddered to think what would happen if he tripped in the aisles between the students' sharp-cornered desks. Or if he were jostled off-balance in the crowded halls at class change. Alan had only one arm to break a fall, and it was not dependable.

My fears were not realized. Without fanfare, Alan's friends carried his books and lunch trays and were careful to perform only whatever other services were necessary. They were a subtle, compassionate fraternity that knew exactly how much help Alan would tolerate.

As the days passed, all of us learned a great deal that wasn't in textbooks. Alan's assignments came in on time. His class participation was thoughtful and sometimes funny. Everyone was a better student because of him . . . and I was a better teacher. If Alan could do it, so could we.

Then suddenly the semester was over, and Alan had earned the credits he needed to graduate.

I have great admiration for the patience Alan exhibited that year in the hospital, at his home, and later in my classroom. Despite the frustration he must have felt over his diminished capabilities, he was never short with me. The only time I heard him speak sharply was when he thought someone threatened his independence.

I'm glad Alan had his senior picture taken before the accident at the end of his junior year. He will one day be able to show it to his children to prove they look just like him.

I'm also glad he and his three best buddies had a group picture made at the junior/senior banquet almost a year later. The scarred, disfigured amputee I had first seen in the hospital room was healing. A glimmer of the old Alan was beginning to emerge. What was inside had never suffered damage. You could always see that in his eyes and in the smile that never left him.

One of the last memories I have of Alan is at his commencement exercise a year after the accident. He had recently undergone another surgery, and his only two fingers were swathed in bandages. There was no hand for the president of the board to shake, no hand to receive the diploma.

A sudden hush fell as Alan mounted the two steps onto the platform, lurched across the stage, and accepted the diploma between his teeth. The crowd went wild as he haltingly managed the two steps down the other side.

That fall he enrolled in a state university. Today—countless surgeries and hours of therapy later—there is every reason to believe he will one day earn the degree he continues to pursue.

All of us whose lives Alan touched during the greatest trial of his life feel we own a special part of him. But he is and always was his own man, and in the end I gained the most. Alan taught me to believe in miracles.

After thirty years in a Hennessey, Oklahoma, high-school classroom, MARJORIE ANDERSON accepted a position as feature writer and columnist with *The Hennessey Clipper*—a weekly newspaper that has served the Hennessey area for 110 years. She continues to live in that small rural community with her dog, who sometimes pinch-hits as author of her weekly column, "I Can't Believe I Said That."

NEAL WEINER

The Mind–Body Problem or My Dog Skippy

Skip bounded ahead
past dangers that lurked behind ferns
and in deep holes between the roots of trees,
while I walked stately down the trail,
pondered meaning and end,
suspecting that his energy
would key for me
the mystery.

Most of all,
he said,
it is to run and lightly touch the ground.
Secondly,
to hear with pricked up ears;
To scratch and snap at flies,
to dig, to catch, sometimes to kill,
to flee big dogs,
snort, sniff, snuff,
to pee where other dogs have peed
and sleep a lot,

which I believed,
every word of it,
without a whiff of condescension
(he would have smelled it instantly;
cut short our conversation)
and now would squirm spine down in earth,
legs spread
shameless,
starblind and joyful,
but one who hears like me
with echo-ears,
who yearns must dream,
must think pale thoughts
and dance with ghosts
to get his barking right.

NEAL WEINER teaches philosophy at Marlboro College, writes poetry, and seeks ways to combine the cognitive power of philosophical logic and poetic sensitivity in the service of spiritual truth. His academic work relates ethics and psychology. Weiner's *The Harmony of the Soul* was published by SUNY, and he is co-author of *The Interstate Gourmet.* He is currently writing a book on language, meaning, and truth.

WALTER R. CHRISTIE

At the Bedside

BEFORE THE FIERY GLOBE OF THE INDIAN SUN RISES above the snowy peaks, its warm yellow light spills down the alpine meadows and over rooftops of the small mountain village of Dharamsala. Eastward beyond the village's wooded ridgeline the Himalayas rise, range after range extending deep into Tibet. Thousands of feet below in the lush Kangra Valley, a white mist, sweet with smoke from morning hearths, slowly rises toward the growing light.

As light intensifies, roof tops buzz with life. Sleepy-eyed monks emerge to perform morning ablutions with basins of collected rainwater. Mothers with baskets snugged to their hips chatter with young children as they drape clean wash on airy clotheslines. On the roof below us, a Western seeker, probably attracted to Dharamsala by the study of Tibetan Buddhism, shakes off the stiffness of travel with a yogic salute to the sun. All around us monkeys scramble up rain spouts and nimbly lope across gutters and roof tiles to position themselves for unguarded pieces of fruit or crusts of morning bread.

Dharamsala, home of the Tibetan government-in-exile, is the location of Men-Tsee-Khang, the Tibetan Medical and Astrological Institute, established by the Dalai Lama to further the teaching and practice of Tibetan Medicine. This morning, along with other Western students, Ellie and I are visiting a small hospital clinic where Tenzin Choedrak, following his morning meditation, is already seeing his first patient. In our lectures Dr. Choedrak has described the methods of Tibetan pulse diagnosis, which allow the physician to discern balance and imbalance in ten organ systems simultaneously. Dr. Choedrak's words alone are not enough. We need to see his fingers sense the surges of a patient's pulse.

Watching with us is a young female medical student who just finished chanting assigned lines from the Four Tantras, the great medical text of Tibetan Medicine. Before she receives her degree she will

*Contemplative
Bodhisattva.*
Limestone, first half sixth
century AD, Lung-men
style, Northern Wei.
9½×16½ in.
Asian Art Museum
of San Francisco.
Gift of Mr. Ed Nagel.
B73 S4.

have memorized all of the Tantras with thousands of diagnoses, treatments, and general advice about health, spiritual practice, and the vicissitudes of the human life cycle. Such orally accessible knowledge will quite naturally enter her mind as she examines each of the thousands of patients she will treat in her lifetime.

Her teacher, Tenzin Choedrak, is a senior faculty member and personal physician to the Dalai Lama. By virtue of his authority, Dr. Choedrak commands great respect, but he needs no title for such recognition. His stature is in his smile, undiminished by twenty-two years in a Chinese prison. As Dr. Choedrak leans to feel the pulse of the young, pregnant Tibetan woman, he offers her his total presence.

Out of respect for the sacred nature of the doctor-patient relationship, the woman has put on her finest dress, carefully braided her hair, and fixed the coil of gathered braids with a fine turquoise comb. Her attractive presentation, however, does not hide her fear, for her face is flushed, and dark circles widen her anxious eyes. This is her second pregnancy. The first ended in miscarriage.

Dr. Choedrak gently holds her wrist. In Tibetan he murmurs to her, then to the student. We think he has told them this may take some time. Both patient and student nod and remain silent. Ellie and I sit to the side, spellbound by the meditative nature of the silence. Minutes pass as Dr. Choedrak feels the pulse. He changes hands, then changes hands again. My mind wanders.

It is a cloudy fall day in 1965, and with four other medical students I am standing in a large, drab male hospital ward where we are about to start a practicum in physical diagnosis. With its faint odor of feces somewhat masked by pungent antiseptics, the ward with its gray walls, tall whitewashed windows, high ceilings, and skeleton of exposed pipes offers a sepulchral atmosphere, more a place of dying than healing. In fact, many of these men, wasted by end-stage cirrhosis or renal failure, will die soon.

It has been a hot summer in Philadelphia in terms of both temperature and racial tensions. Only a year ago sections of the city were in flames, and the fires of social change continue to smolder in the blocks around the medical school. The poor people's caravan to Washington is yet to come as well as the assassination of Robert Kennedy and Martin Luther King. We draftable medical students are thinking about Vietnam, but not as much as we will before we graduate in 1968. Outside the opaque windows cars honk at pedestrians, anxiously making their way across the infamous treachery of Broad Street.

I hardly notice the roar of the streets or the rising politics in the poverty-ridden blocks around the hospital. The larger world is only a dim reality, for success this morning demands that I give all my attention to my teacher, Dr. Miller, a specialist in internal medicine, selected to instruct five of us in methods of chest percussion and auscultation.

As we students crowd around, Dr. Miller positions himself at the cranked-up bed of Mr. Jones, an African American man in his fifties. Mr. Jones' johnny is untied, and he bends his bare back forward to allow Dr. Miller to tap lightly along the bottom of his ribs. As Mr. Jones breathes, Dr. Miller cocks the second finger of his right hand, fashioning it into a small hammer. With quick flips of his wrist he thumps the fingertip against the patient's chest wall. I listen intently. From one side of Mr. Jones' chest comes a nice deep resonant note while the other offers a muffled flat dead sound.

Dr. Miller gazes at us as if to say, Do you know what these sounds mean? Remarkably I do. Indeed, their quality is almost magical, for upon hearing them I can see in my mind's eye the viscous froth dulling the lobe of Mr. Jones' lung. Light percussion of the human chest is a simple thing, yet the sounds convey such direct, useful knowledge.

"Breathe deeply, Mr. Jones!" Dr. Miller says.

As Mr. Jones breathes, the area of dullness rises and falls. Again I marvel that so much can be known.

"Now, Mr. Christie, you try," Dr. Miller says and steps aside to allow me access to my patient.

"The students will each examine you," Dr. Miller says. His voice is firm, but friendly.

As a boy I dreaded visits to the doctor, so this morning as I anticipated examining my first patient, I expected that he or she would experience me with feelings ranging from mild irritation to marked perturbation or outright affront. Yet, strangely, as each of us tap his chest, Mr. Jones seems engaged and relaxed, almost grateful for our efforts as if the laying on of many hands accentuates his healing process.

This transformation of Mr. Jones' awkward nudity and our fumbling hands into a healing event is quite remarkable. Somehow Dr. Miller, through his voice and touch, has established an atmosphere at the bedside that encircles all of us in a healing covenant. This is no longer just the perspiration soaked bedside of a sick man in a dreary ward of dying men, but instead is healing temenos, a place of caring and ultimate concern, demanding the full intelligence and attention of us new physicians. By asking us to join our minds and hands on the patient's body at the bedside, Dr. Miller has begun a teaching/healing process that initiates us to our medical careers. As I tentatively percuss Mr. Jones' back and feel his damp feverish skin, I immediately become his doctor.

When Dr. Choedrak sits with his patient, the sacred dimension of the doctor–patient relationship is defined by Tibetan Buddhist practice as the place where each person one meets is potentially the Buddha. Thus, in daily meditation Dr. Choedrak and other Tibetan physicians cultivate the Medicine Buddha in themselves and work to encounter the Buddha in each patient, even when they must see a hundred patients a day.

In fact, Buddhist beliefs define more than just the doctor–patient dyad. Dr. Dawa, another of our teachers in Dharamsala, signed a folio of his drawings of medicinal herbs with the reminder "Everything is medicine." For the Tibetans this is literally true. All food, climate, sunlight, exercise, meditation, prayer, laughter, and tears are medicinal. Tibetan doctors, thus, must treat all life reverentially and must take excellent care of themselves in order to remain allied with good medicine.

However, in 1965 when I first percussed Mr. Jones' chest, centuries had passed since mainstream Western medicine held beliefs of the unity of mind, body, and environment similar to those of the Tibetans. Although ancient Greek medicine, holistically fathered by Hippocrates and sacramentally mediated by the healing god Asclepius, is the foundation of our Western medicine, by the Middle Ages application of medical knowledge had degenerated into a relatively uninformed secular practice, and the healing power of spirit had become the sole property of the clergy.

When Dr. Miller stood by Mr. Jones' bed and invited us to percuss his chest, he held no sense of the sacred, no consciousness of the presence of Buddha or the god Asclepius, perhaps just a recollection of the Hippocratic Oath he had sworn upon graduation from medical school. In retrospect, however, I see that Asclepius/Buddha was there, for when medicine is done well, the bedside becomes both a classroom and a temple, a circle of healing where doctor, patient, health, and illness are enclosed in a field of spiritual forces.

Today in Dharamsala, Dr. Choedrak relies on his senses and a contemplative mind to divine the nature of the subtle imbalances underlying his patients' illnesses. For him and for other physicians of holistic pre-scientific traditional cultures, the fundamental condition of the bedside—the direct sensate, mental, spiritual, energetic relationship of doctor with patient—remains the core of the practice. But in the West, embracing postmodern positivist thinking, we tend to characterize such holistic views as naive and outmoded.

Unwittingly, Western physicians desacralize healing and identify the skills of the bedside only with modern procedures (inserting IV lines, performing bone marrow aspirations) that occur in certain places (hospitals, clinics, physicians' offices). Sometimes before treatment begins there is no moment of professional intimacy, no methodical history-taking or thorough examination of the body, just check-in receptions, speedy venipuncturists, whirlwind X-ray techs, and strange rides through the unreal corridors of surgical suites.

In Dharamsala Dr. Choedrak lets the young woman's wrist sink to her lap. In Tibetan he advises her about diet and exercise, and then in a quick scrawl he writes a prescription for a herbal pill. The patient thanks him, presses her hands together in a gesture of "Namaste," and leaves. Dr. Choedrak smiles briefly at us before rising to greet the next patient, an old man with a bent spine. In this patient Dr. Choedrak expects to meet the Buddha as well.

After Dr. Choedrak has treated the old man, Ellie and I leave the clinic and join a stream of villagers descending and ascending the path along the ridgeline. In the growing morning light, snow glints a brilliant white on the peaks above Dharamsala. Headed toward their morning studies, monks and nuns in red and gold robes smile at us as we walk upward toward our small hotel. Enjoying the walk, Ellie and I talk about our experience at Men-Tsee-Khang, and we confess feeling a little foolish, for we came to Dharamsala with typical Western expectations of extracting the essence of Tibetan medicine in just three weeks. Instead, we stand humbled by the highly conscious, moral Tibetan culture, and we realize that its holistic methods cannot be lifted from their Asian context and transported back home for Western consumption. We also talk about our time with Dr. Choedrak and the good fortune to be in the presence of an inspiring teacher who offers us a model of mindfulness, diligence, and patience—qualities most lacking in our busy Western practices.

Stopping before a vista of wooded mountainsides dotted with monasteries, we gaze for a moment, and I tell Ellie that I feel especially grateful for our time in Dharamsala. Without consciously seeking it, I notice a subtle change in my sense of what it means to be a medical practitioner. It seems that when my memory of examining Mr. Jones arose in the context of observing the mindfulness, vitality, and integrity of Dr. Choedrak's care of his patients, I was once again initiated as a physician, and I glimpsed the sacramental dimension of medical work that lies at the root of all medical traditions—East and West. Surprisingly, this deeper understanding did not come by witnessing some miraculous healing, but through observing simple moments of respectful care. Watching Dr. Choedrak was a reminder of the archetypal intimacy and mystery of the unique spiritual domain where physicians do their work—at the bedside.

WALTER R. CHRISTIE, MD, FAPA, is an attending psychiatrist in the outpatient division of Maine Medical Center. In addition to clinical work, Dr. Christie supervises residents and teaches medical students from the University of Vermont Medical School where he is an associate clinical professor. In 1995 Dr. Christie and his wife Elinor studied medicine in India at the Dalai Lama's medical school in Dharamsala. The Christies have subsequently hosted Tibetan physicians visiting the United States.

PART V

Beyond the Classroom

Vacations

When I went down to Cooperstown
The house was on the street.
The rooms stood still
And I told Will
That all the shoes had feet.

When we drove into Bennington
The mountains all had trees.
And I told Kate
(Though we were late)
That every pod had peas.

When we got up to Biddeford
The sea was in the air.
And I told Lou
(Who's only two)
That I could smell it there.

When I came back to Boston
The grass was on the ground.
And do you know
I think it's so
The wide world round.

—JULIA RANDALL

ROSALIND BAKER WILSON

Dining with the Dos Passos

A Lesson in Hospitality

I REMEMBER THE MOST COVETED INVITATION TO DINNER among the inhabitants of lower Cape Cod, Provincetown, Truro, and Wellfleet, was to be asked to John and Katy Dos Passos' house at 375 Commercial Street in Provincetown—until Katy's death in a car accident in 1946. After which, Dos, one of the giants of American literature, moved away.

From the time I became aware of dinner parties when I was eight or so, until I was twenty-three and the Dos Passos' ghastly accident, it was The Invitation.

The food was excellent, but looking back, that was not the only reason it was such a delightful prospect. They made their own time and space for dinner, which took place at eight o'clock and was always preceded by tea, which began at five or so. That end of the Cape, with its accumulation of artists and dash of successful summering doctors, had some very competitive cooks. The Dosses, however, were perpetual winners in the dinner sweepstakes.

The house at the east end of Provincetown had its back and Dos's adored vegetable garden on the harbor. You entered through the front with a pretty flower garden surrounded by a high picket fence. Not a blade of grass grew between the fence and Commercial Street. Once through the front door, you were in a room running the full length of the house, a fireplace at the street end, a superb view of the

Opposite:
Edwin Dickinson
View from Dos' Window.
Graphite on paper,
10x13 in., 1936.
Provincetown Art
Association and
Museum, Provincetown,
Massachusetts.

harbor and Long Point Lighthouse at the other end. There were pretty little antique sofas with suitably sized tables scattered around the room, and one great, deep couch for the more sedentary guests.

Katy, whose maiden name was Smith, her brother, and her best friend, Edith Foley, had owned and lived in the house before Katy's marriage to Dos and Edith's to Frank Shay. Katherine Smith and Edith Foley wrote many best-selling books about Cape Cod and a best-selling novel, *Captain Smith.* Among items in his own distinguished vita, Frank had compiled a successful cookbook *The Best Men Are Cooks.* The house had been named Smooley Hall, a combination of Smith and Foley, and that name stuck through the years after Katy's marriage to Dos.

The Smooley group had kept a barrel in the great room into which they poured apple juice, tossed orange and lemon peels, raisins, and yeast. It was known as The Boy. People who drank from it were energized for days; and one Boston doctor-beau of Katy's started recommending it to his patients.

A modified version of The Boy was maintained by Dos and Katy in the dark closet downstairs off the dining room with a few remaining bottles of Prohibition Tiger Cat whiskey, which had somehow turned out deep and rich.

A ladder-like set of stairs went down to the dining room and kitchen on the bottom floor. There were stucco walls in the dining room and an austere fireplace, and little windows looking up to the garden, and a back entrance. The dining room had a refectory table with straight-backed Shaker chairs. The kitchen had a gas stove, vegetable bins, and an old-fashioned Frigidaire with one of those apparatus on top that looked like a stack of oversized dinner plates, and a great tin sink. The downstairs floors were flagstone.

Some people feel the best way to give a dinner party is to have everything ready beforehand, so you can relax and enjoy the guests. The Dosses functioned on the opposite principle, not letting the dinner preparations interfere with their day. That was principle one. Principle two, they believed tea and drinks should be served simultaneously.

Sometimes people would be invited in advance; sometimes they would just drop in. The Dosses had no children of their own, and I was part of what Dos called Katy's Youth Movement. I would show up with some college friend or beau. On one occasion or another, my friends and I may have been walking around Great Island in Wellfleet (which we loved to do with nothing but an oyster knife, a pocket knife, a couple of lemons, and a bottle of white wine mit corkscrew.) "Oh oysters, dear, a little walk, a little talk," we'd chant from Lewis Carroll's "The Walrus and the Carpenter" as we picked up the innocent bivalves and ate them on the spot. If we had an old sweater, jeans, or a large bath towel, we'd tie some oysters up and take them to the Dosses.

If the conversation became hot and heavy over drinks, the Dosses would opt for Oysters Rockefeller instead of opening myriad oysters by hand—although we regarded the alternative as somewhat corrupt.

A Dos Passos day was getting up at five, writing until eleven, lunching, perhaps working in his vegetable garden between the house and steps down to the harbor. They might take a trip in their rowboat or a long walk, ambling into the house around five-thirty or so, and start preparing the tea, served in the long, street-floor room with a display of Limoges and crystal. Dos would circle the room, gently holding the tea pot in which My Lord Earl Grey resided, gently rotating it as the tea steeped for seven room-circles. Katy would surface from below with toasted Portuguese sweet bread and a bowl of opaque white-clover honey, which they ordered in large cans from a western apiary. Drinks were served with some cheesy accompaniment, cheese on Rye Krisp with a dash of Worcestershire hot from the oven. Perhaps Portuguese white bread with cucumber and dill and cream cheese.

The Portuguese baker had a no-nonsense, immaculate shop in which he baked white and sweet bread and sold flipper dough. Nothing else. The bread, the white in plump wide oval loaves and the sweet in round loaves, still seems to me to surpass any other.

During the tea between political controversy or tales of Dos's latest assignment and journey—one of which had been to interview MacArthur in the Philippines, whom Dos described as did General Eisenhower, as one of our greatest living actors—the Dosses would decide what to have for dinner and mosey around getting it. Very often it was fish that their neighbor, Charlie Mayo, a famous sailor, brought them from the wharves.

Fish was still often free in those days. The fishermen tossed it to people as they came in from the traps in the morning—perhaps mackerel, from which Dos would make a salad. He baked it at high heat for ten minutes, then let it rest in brandy for half an hour. The fishermen called tuna horse mackerel. The mackerel salad seemed better than tuna salad, more delicate. Perhaps it was the herbs, tomatoes with a dash of cinnamon, or because I had on occasion been out to the traps with the fishermen and had seen how the highly prized tuna were bludgeoned to death, while the mackerel were so small they were hauled in and eventually died gasping but unbloodied. Sometimes someone appeared with a sea bass caught on a line on the Back Shore, as the ocean side of the Cape was known.

Katy would make Cape Cod Turkey, stuffing it with Portuguese bread and a touch of linguicia, a spicy Portuguese sausage cut very fine. The whole thing was accompanied by small pieces of gently sauteed flipper dough in lieu of potatoes. There were the vegetables from Dos's garden, a favorite—green peppers stuffed with spinach laced with nutmeg. For dessert, sometimes a modified version of one I'd introduced from my grandmother's menus, orange sections covered with soft custard topped with dabs of soft meringue. The Dosses added Cointreau. They did their basic shopping while the guests were there, calling up Birches Market down the street to deliver butter, milk, whatever was needed.

No one got drunk at the Dos Passos dinners. There was none of the tenseness or sloppiness of people who decide to invite you to dinner after the fifth martini. You just seemed to feel cozy and warm as you gradually coasted from tea to dinner, from the Limoges to the sturdy peasant Mexican shallow-bowl dinner plates on which dinner was served.

Looking back, it's amazing no one ever slipped down the ladder stairway to the dining room. The Dosses were nimble-footed as mountain goats, with no mishaps. Katy was very amusing about cooking and took it lightly. Once I spent the night and found Katy beating up milk for breakfast café au lait to make it foamy and more exciting. "I tried," she said, "but only I am foaming!"

After dinner, the party moved back upstairs for coffee and thick, sweet bourbon (sometimes the precious Tiger Cat) served in liqueur glasses. Hadn't Frank Shay in *The Best Men Are Cooks* laid down the law: The best post-dinner liqueur is a heavy bourbon? There was no after-dinner drinking other than that small glass. There never seemed to be any clutter or mess. Maybe the austerity of the kitchen and dining room had something to do with it and the fact they were separate floors.

The tea/dinner-drink combo, the relaxed attitude of the hosts to entertaining, and the camaraderie of their happy marriage, all made the atmosphere an ambiance unto the Dosses themselves.

ROSALIND BAKER WILSON, former editor at Houghton Mifflin and author of stories and memoirs, died near Talcottville, New York, in October 2000. Her book *Near the Magician: A Memoir of My Father, Edmund Wilson* (1989) describes life as the oldest child of the famous American critic, editor, and author. Rosalind's ashes were scattered in Sugar River, just beyond the old Stone House where her father spent his summers and where Rosalind loved to swim.

DINO ADKINS

The Education of William Page

Painting Soul into Canvas and America's Entry into Modern Art

AT THE AGE OF THIRTY-NINE, William Page (1811–1885) set out for Europe. Ever since his early training with Samuel F.B. Morse, Page's dream had been to travel to Rome. For American artists of the mid-nineteenth century, it was a breathtaking experience to walk on Italian soil in the footsteps of Michelangelo, Raphael, Titian, and Augustus.[1] Like many American artists, Page yearned for an inner circle of artists where ideas were nurtured and where the comings of the Industrial Age were not held in the highest priority. During the 1840s and 1850s, Rome became an American artists' colony insulated from the trappings and interruptions of Western society. Page describes the environment:

> No talk of money here; no discussion of public measure; no conversation respecting new enterprises, and the ebb and flow of trade; no price current, except of marble and canvas; all the talk is of art and of artists.[2]

Chronologically, there is little contiguous detail available on William Page's day-to-day experiences in Europe, but his travel can be summarized. In late 1849, he embarked for the European continent aboard a vessel of the Grinnell and Minturn line, and, after thirty-one days sailing, he landed at Dover and immediately set across the channel to Calais, having his first stay of length in Paris for six weeks. Afterwards, he set for Marseilles, then Nice, and passing through Genoa en route to Florence where he would live for three

Aphrodite.
Marble. Greek,
fifth century, B.C.
The British Museum.

years. During this time, he would travel throughout the Tuscan landscape, seeing all that he could and spending an entire summer in
Venice. From Florence, he would finally reach Rome where he would
live for the remainder of his stay in Europe excepting for a summer's
vacation in London between 1851–1858 and a few weeks in New
York in the fall of 1858.

THROUGH THE FIRST HALF OF THE NINETEENTH CENTURY, American art had been steeped in the classical tradition, and Page at that time was devoted to the values of antiquity. Early in his development, he believed nature to be the basis for art, and classicism was the glorifying story of its beauty. From the Louvre, the Medici Palace, the Vatican, and the British Museum, he studied and absorbed the details of sculptures and images from ancient times. Molded by his religious upbringing and by his years as a seminary student, Page felt that what God endowed could not be enhanced by a generous paint stroke or a benevolent chisel. Nature's design was pristine, and any attempt to circumvent that design was blasphemy. And yet, although he thought of nature as perfect, he believed that for many of his peers, art had become a soulless pursuit for this perfection. In comparing periods of art and artists, he was quick to distinguish between what is nature and imbued with a soul, and what is stylized idealism. At the British Museum he measured and studied Greek sculpture, giving special attention to the Elgin and Towneley marbles which he considered the "highest 'angels' of sculpture that the world has known."[3]

From these studies of classical sculpture, he defined and developed theories about the painting process and a well structured and defined system of proportions for the human figure, a natural standard. He cited the provenance for his theorem from scriptures: "And he measured the wall thereof, an hundred and forty and four cubits, according to the measure of a man, that is, of the angel."[4] This geometry combined with classical sculpture established the basis of the system. For over twenty years, he studied the dynamics of the human figure, and his calculations repeatedly coincided with the above notation and other numerics in the Old and New Testaments. This method squared the human figure into a cruciform measuring twelve by twelve units, for example, the same number of apostles and gates into heaven.[5]

Page found that Greek sculpture adhered to his system of proportions. He stated, "This is not the standard of Canova or of Thorwalsen, or even of the *Apollo Belvedere*, but it is the standard of Phidias and of the remains of the Parthenon."[6] Upon returning to America, he wrote, "A New Geometrical Mode of Measuring the Proportions of the Human Body, Verified by the Best Greek Art,"[7] and then later in a more concise article, "The Measure of a Man."[8]

A Shaken Ideal

Dino Adkins

IT WAS DURING THIS PERIOD, HOWEVER, THAT PAGE STOPPED believing in all classical sculpture as a general art standard and began to build a selective aesthetic with Greek Classicism as the foundation. It was his first step towards assigning meaning without tradition, a transition to modern art. According to Page, because the Elgin Marbles were created within an aesthetic prescribing a divine naturalism, qualified by Page's system of proportions, they became unique. By definition, Page had little choice in selecting an antique source for his paintings, of which there were many. Page's reasoning for choosing the Elgin Marbles or Greek sculpture over the *Apollo* or *Torso Belvedere* or other Roman sculpture, for example, was essentially an act of modern reasoning. Michelangelo was known to have referred to the *Torso Belvedere* as one of the greatest works ever, but to Page, the sculpture was imperfect because it did not adhere, stylistically, to his system of proportions as prescribed by the scriptures. Because the *Torso Belvedere* and related works were ideal and not imbued stylistically with a soul, they could not have a soul and, therefore, he felt could not be art.

A New Aesthetic

RETURNING TO AMERICA, Page wrote, "No idea has ever been presented to the world in such a variety of number of forms as that of a spirit, or goddess, of love and beauty."[9] He was so taken by this notion that he painted *Venus Rising from the Sea* and three versions of *Venus Guiding Eneas and the Trojans to the Latin Shore* of which one painting survives. Venus is central within the vertical canvas standing astride a half-shell gently propelled on either side by two putti. At Venus' feet are two doves who tow the shell with red ribbon. A reflection of the group can be seen in the foreground. In the background, a convoy of galleys is seen following, in deference to Venus's lead.

Beginning with this canvas, Page separates himself from the academic tradition by bringing together three influences: Greek Classical Sculpture, Color Theory, and Swedenborgianism, which he had been introduced to in Florence (where there was a group of artists, including the Brownings and Hiram Powers, who read Swedenborg together). From first glance at this painting, the viewer is compelled by the moving elegant scene. Standing before us unclothed and unabashed, Venus is open but not naked. She is tempered by the tools of his newfound spirituality. By Page's own admission, the basis for this work is an antique torso in the British Museum (page 150). Page considered this work from the fifth cen-

tury B.C.E. a hallmark of classical sculpture and of art in general. Venus was based on a Greek work because Page felt only Greek works had a soul, and thus only they could provide the life-giving heartbeat for something akin to God creating man.

As a dedicated student of Titian, Page uses color to imbue this classical image with his own spirit. Color is part of the message. Page had long been an exponent of the oil-glazing technique, and while he rendered Venus using this method, he completely changed the impetus. For example, when painting the appearance of a vein just under the skin, it was important to Page to not simply paint a pale blue line within the flesh tone. Instead he painted a red vein within the flesh tone (because blood is red) and then used layers of glaze to render the red vein blue. Likewise, Page painted Venus using layer upon layer of glaze as if to create a being from within as God had created man. As a result, Page had striven to create the same flesh-tone as Titian, whom he considered a colorist master above all others, with an intent to paint his soul into the canvas.

After learning about the Swedish scientist and mystic Emanuel Swedenborg (1688–1772),[10] Page became imbued with Swedenborg's system of three spheres, divine mind, spiritual world, natural world, each corresponding to a state of being: love, wisdom, and use. Through devotion to these states an individual could achieve his or her destiny, which is the fusion of creator and creation. This new doctrine said that true art echoes nature's splendor but also includes a spirit unique among creations. In every created thing there are three elements: end, cause, and effect. The end identifies itself with God, the cause is the formulation in the spirit world, and the effect is the perceivable form in nature.[11] Applied to art, the *end* is the artist's initial conception, the *cause* relates to the material at his disposal, and the *effect* is the work itself incorporating the artist's soul.[12] Page arrived in Europe with a strong belief in God and the Holy Bible and equally stout aesthetics in technique. His cloudy vision between the two was now defined through this new spirituality as he began to rethink the entire creative process.

This rethinking process was coming during a pivotal period in William Page's life. His career had undergone the typical doubt and maturing of a struggling artist, but his personal life was in constant tumult. Earlier, in 1832 at the age of twenty-one, Page had married Lavinia Twibill, and while the marriage produced three daughters, it was ill-fated and ended in divorce in 1840. During the marriage, Page was never able to consistently secure commissions for portraits and was usually penniless so that the Pages were supported in large part by Lavinia's family. This caused emotional hardship between him and his wife. The desolation of the marriage was so painful to Page

Opposite:
William Page.
Mrs. William Page.
Oil on canvas,
55×85¾ in.,
1860–1861.
Detroit Institute of Arts.
Gift of Mr. and Mrs.
George S. Page,
Blinn S. Page,
Lowell Briggs Page,
and Mrs. Leslie Stockton
Howell.

that some thirty years later, he would recount that Lavinia had actually died rather than admit to the divorce.[13] Later in 1840, Page would remarry, to Sara Dougherty, an actress of some fame and beauty. While in Rome, this marriage too would end. In the fall of 1858, Page left Rome and returned to New York for a few weeks. The purpose of this trip was singular: to obtain a divorce from his second wife, Sara Dougherty. Sara had abandoned Page and his teenage daughters from his previous marriage. What Page could not forget (nor would the press or public let him forget) was that Sara had eloped with an Italian count. The Italian police had brought her back, and though Page pleaded with her to stay, she left him permanently. Early in 1859, Page remarried yet again to a widow and American correspondent, Sophia Candace Stevens Hitchcock. Sophia publicly hesitated in marrying the now 48-year-old Page. But they did in fact marry and had six children. During this time, Page had little to rely upon. He was usually given to the generosity of others, his humiliation from Sara's elopement never left him, and above all else, he was completely reevaluating his role as an artist.

Page's best known paintings are his *Self Portrait* and *Sophia Candace Stevens Hitchcock Page,* both of which were begun in Rome and completed in New York. The *Self Portrait* is a vertical canvas with Page standing in the foreground wearing a vest and housecoat. From his studio in Rome, he is looking away and to his right while in his hands he holds the tools of his trade, a palette with brushes and a bracing staff in his left hand and a bristle brush held in the fingertips of his right hand. The horizon is established by his spectacles which dangle at waist height from a cord hanging around his neck, encircling his body. His gaze is in the same direction as the figure of Theseus from the Parthenon pediment who reclines behind him.

In the portrait of his third wife, *Sophia Candace Stevens Hitchcock Page,* the pose is similar but the scene is outdoors taken from the *Via Sacra* and manipulated in a manner to build a collective scene rather than reproduce the view. The Colosseum and surrounding remains are lyrically reconstructed with the form of the Colosseum framing Mrs. Page's face and bonnet. The fragments in the middle ground orchestrate a rhythm echoed by her voluminous skirt. Again, as with Venus previously, Page combines the past with a new sensibility. He uses the Roman remains as a foundation and rearranges the view to build a new scene with meaning. This step into constructing a composition rather than reproducing reality shows Page's interest in moving beyond the academic tradition.

By using classical sculpture as the foundation for a painting that documents beauty or the ideal, Page embraced the American art of his generation. But when he embedded a sense of spirit or soul into the canvas, a soul disguised by tradition and classical mystique, he launched into modern art. Like God creating man with beauty determined by an underlying truth or soul, the artist chooses a subject based in nature but filled with the soul of the artist, giving the work a unique and profound meaning. William Page looked behind a veil of academic tradition for an inward creative force. He entered the European landscape viewing tradition as a hallmark of skill, intellect, and classical exuberance. But he left as modern artist.

DINO ADKINS has been museum director at various institutions and presently is director of Edwards Place Historic Home and Galleries in Springfield, Illinois. His speciality is history of nineteenth-century American art, with his undergraduate work in art history and photography at Ohio University and graduate training in art history and museum administration at George Washington University and the Smithsonian Institution. Dr. Adkins is a painter and photographer, and is completing a book of photography and writing, *Through the Florida Myst.*

Notes

1. Taylor, Joshua. *William Page: The American Titian.* University of Chicago Press, 1957. pp. 102–103.

2. From a letter quoting Bryant, dated May 21, 1858, reprinted in *Crayon,* Volume V (1858), p. 202–203.

3. Page, William. "The Measure of a Man", *Scribner's Monthly,* XVII, p. 895.

4. *The Holy Bible,* New Testament, Book of Revelation, Chapter 21, verse 17, King James Version.

5. Page, William. "The Measure of a Man", *Scribner's Monthly,* XVII, p. 896.

6. *Ibid.,* p. 898 (Antonio Canova, (1757–1822), Italy), (Bertel Thorwaldsen, (1768–1884), Holland).

7. To date, a published edition of this article has not been located but a copy of the transcript is in The Page Papers in The Archives of American Art, Smithsonian Institution, Washington, D.C.

8. Page, William. "The Measure of a Man", *Scribner's Monthly,* XVII (1879), p. 896.

9. ———. *Venus Guiding Eneas and the Trojans to the Latin Shore.* p. 1.

10. Page had been introduced to the biblical interpretations of Emanuel Swedenborg while living in Florence by the American sculptor Hiram Powers and by Thomas Worcester, the minister of the Boston New Jerusalem Church who was in Florence at the time. Silver, Richard. "Spirit in American Art: The Image as Hieroglyph." *Emanuel Swedenborg: A Continuing Vision.* Robin Larsen ed., New York: Swedenborg Foundation, 1988, p. 67.

11. Taylor, Joshua. *William Page, The American Titian.* Chicago: University of Chicago Press, 1957, p. 223.

12. *Ibid.,* p. 223.

13. Townley, D.O.C., "Living American Artists: William Page", *Scribner's Monthly,* III (1872), p. 602.

MARIAN CHARLES

In Movies, Blond and Thin Is Best

Let's go to the opera instead.
The heroine is fifty and weighs
as much as a '65 Chevy with fins.
She could crack your jaw in her fist.
She can hit high C lying down.

The tenor the women scream for
wolfs an eight course meal daily.
He resembles a bull on hind legs.
His thighs the size of beer kegs.
His chest is a redwood with hair.

The hippopotamus baritone (the villain)
has a voice that could give you
an orgasm right in your seat.
His voice smokes with passion.
He is hot as lava. He erupts nightly.

The contralto is, however, svelte.
She is supposed to be the soprano's
other, but is ten years younger,
beautiful and black. Nobody cares.
She sings you into her womb where you rock.

Their voices twine, golden serpents.
Their voices rise like the best
fireworks and hang and hang
then drift slowly down descending
in brilliant and still fiery sparks.
Let's go to the opera instead.

MARIAN CHARLES is a registered nurse in Rapid City, South Dakota, with degrees in nursing, biology, and art. She has always loved classical music and wrote this poem after watching an opera on television. An accomplished artist, she has many artworks on display in her area.

THOMAS F. WILLIAMS

One Hour

HIS FATHER HAD SAID IT WOULD BE GOOD EXPERIENCE, and his mother had not said anything one way or the other. John had been out of high school for a month, and though he was not yet seventeen, the only sensible thing to do was to get a job and start being a man. If you were under eighteen, it was impossible to find work in a factory, so his father had contacted someone who arranged the door-to-door sales job with World-Wide Paper Products at twenty-five percent straight commission.

He had tried selling magazines when he was twelve until one day a man who was mad at his wife rushed out the door and told John to get the hell off his front porch. He had quit that job. Now he was starting back in the selling business again. Not much of a start, he thought.

But everybody started that way, his father said; and anyhow you had to work.

Maybe in a little while he and Rosalee could begin to live the way Rosalee was sure people ought to live. Then, they would go wherever they wanted to—horseback riding, and swimming at the right places in the summer. Places where there would be a dance pavilion hanging over the water with a great band and champagne bottles popping. Rosalee was a knockout in a bathing suit and was always happy thinking about a big brick house in St. Louis with a terrace and a double garage, and maybe they would play golf. They would dance and play golf and swim and live together for God knows how many years because at sixteen it looks like a long time before you're old.

John was thinking of these things instead of listening to Mr. Curtis who stood beside him on the corner of 25th and Audubon Streets. Mr. Curtis was a field manager for Worldwide Paper Products and he was explaining how John ought to handle the customers in his new territory. "Now you've got it all straight, haven't you?"

"I think so," John answered. "I just knock on the door, and when they let me in I show them all the stuff and talk them into something."

"Thatsa boy. Talk to them. That's the main thing. Talk their heads off before they get a chance to shake them." Mr. Curtis laughed nervously at his favorite remark and patted John on the shoulder. Mr. Curtis was shorter than John and coat-hanger thin. His face twitched as he talked, and his legs and arms seemed always to be moving even when he was standing in place. "Well, I've got to be going now. Lots of work to do. Meet you at the end of the block in about an hour to see how you've made out."

"Okay, Mr. Curtis."

"So long," Mr. Curtis said over his shoulder as he trotted off in the direction of his dark brown company sedan parked mid-block.

Theodore J. Roszak.
Emergence: Transition I..
Steel and bronze,
38×48½×21 cm., 1945.
Arizona State University
Museum, Tempe.
Gift of Oliver B. James.

John leaned over and picked up the artificial leather suitcase that held the latest line of Worldwide Paper Products. It was one in the afternoon in July in East St. Louis and very hot. He began walking toward his first house in a straight block of squat one-story houses. The weight of the suitcase pulled on the muscles of his neck. He cocked his head to the left and walked toward the first house, the suitcase knocking against his knee, his thin wrists straining from the already too-short sleeves of his graduation jacket. Across the street the wind tousled the top branches of a long row of poplar trees. Their dusty leaves rattled dryly against one another and dropped a blotch of shade close to each of their trunks.

The heat pressed up steadily from the white cement. John's collar stuck against the back of his neck, and his fingers were slippery around the suitcase grip. He stood on the steps of the first house now, looking through black, rust-spotted screens at a front porch that was streaked with shafts of sunlight and square shadows of warm shade. He doubled his fist to knock on the screen door, but his arm refused to move. Then he felt a sick revolt against the whole plan. Running down the steps as though someone were chasing him, he didn't stop until he was across the street under one of the poplar trees. He had begun to perspire more heavily, and the heat was throbbing against his throat. To hell with it, he said to himself. To hell with it. Part of his mind told him to hide for an hour, and when Mr. Curtis showed up, tell him to shove his black suitcase into the trunk of his Worldwide Products automobile, and that would end it. But the sensible part of his mind granted no importance to that fantasy, so in a few minutes he rubbed his handkerchief over his face and started back to the first house again. He knocked weakly against the screen door. The sound of his knocking seemed to trail disturbingly over all the houses in the neighborhood, and he half hoped that no one would answer. After waiting awhile he opened the screen door and stepped onto the porch. He pushed the doorbell and waited, and felt his warm breath swelling against the back of his palate.

The door opened. "Yes?" asked a thin, pale woman, staring into his face.

"Madam," John said in the formal tone of the piece he had memorized, "I should be very much interested in showing you the latest line in Worldwide Products. I'm sure you will find something that will interest you and at the same time prove ..."

"I see," the woman interrupted in a high, gentle voice. "Come on in, and let's see what you're selling."

John picked up the suitcase and followed the woman through a low-ceilinged vestibule. They stopped in the over-crowded living room where the woman pointed toward one of the chairs, and John sat down. The woman sat on a davenport across from him, and with her elbows on her knees and her fists doubled under her chin, she leaned forward and looked at him. The shades were drawn, and the room was dark and cool. John wanted to lean back and rest, but the woman was waiting for him to begin. He reached down and un-latched the black suitcase, spreading it open to display a tight-packed collection of paper products. Wall dusters, mops, sponges, napkins, table cloths, and dozens of other items, all made of Worldwide Paper.

"As you can see, Madam . . ." he began.

"Yes, yes." The woman interrupted in her wispy voice. "My, I never knew there was so many things made from paper. What's that little red thing in the corner?"

"That's a gift set of bridge coasters."

"It is?"

"Yes, ma'am."

"Well, I don't know," the woman said. "I don't know what I really need. It's really a scorcher today, isn't it?"

"Yes, ma'am, it's pretty hot. Do you think you might like . . ."

"Well, I don't know what I'd like. I'll just have to see everything."

"Lou!" a man shouted from somewhere in the back of the house. He was heading toward the living room. John could hear his voice coming closer. "Lou, get off your dead can and find me a clean shirt." He stood sideways in the arched doorway across the room, and though he hadn't yet noticed John, John could see that he was huge; his stomach formed a lumped ridge above the belt of his work pants and little streams of sweat ran down arms the size of hams, soaking an already stained undershirt.

The woman looked at the floor and got up quickly. "I'm sorry, but there's not a thing I need."

"Who in the hell are you talking to?" the husband asked.

"There's a young man here, selling paper products," she answered in her soft, apologetic voice, hurrying, and looking very small as she passed her husband, to disappear into the back of the house.

"I didn't see you sitting there," the man said to John. "Did my wife act like she was going to buy something?" he laughed.

"How do you do," John said. He closed the suitcase and got up from the chair.

"She wasn't going to buy anything," the man went on. "She wasn't going to buy anything because I don't give her any money." He laughed hard as though he had made a great joke. "She just wants to talk to people. She talks to everybody that walks by the house, but she never buys anything because she hasn't got any money." The man laughed again. "You better go someplace else, kid."

"Well, good afternoon," John said as he walked through the vestibule.

"Goodbye, kid."

He was out on the sidewalk again. His head felt disorganized and light, and he decided to rest for a minute before going on to the next house. He sat under a tree on the big suitcase, and Rosalee's dream floated into his mind, mixed with the idea he was still adjusting to, that he was out of high school and a man now. Being a man was already beginning to be complicated. Because he was not yet seventeen and had disliked all the work he had ever done, John had the notion that you lived only when you were not working or sleeping. Eight hours to sleep, eight hours to work, and sometimes part of the eight living hours you had to spend doing things that were a waste of time. It didn't seem right.

He picked up the suitcase. It was pulling hard on his shoulder and rubbing the skin from his leg. He walked unevenly, one leg taking longer strides than the other, past a weed-tangled vacant lot where insects flew and hopped and hummed in the thick heat of the afternoon. At the second house he was almost to the porch when he was stopped by an old man sitting in the shade of a small tree in the front yard.

"What are you peddlin', boy?"

"I'm selling Worldwide Paper Products," John answered.

"Pretty good line?" the old man asked. He sat holding his puffed stomach. His lips were wrinkled over his sunken mouth and dark tobacco spittle clung to one side of his gray stubbled chin. He looked at John as if John amused him very much.

"Yes, this is a good product," John said. "This company is one of the foremost paper manufacturing concerns in the world."

"Yes, yes, I don't doubt it," the old man answered. "I know that company. Makes everything from you-know-what to Christmas cards." He laughed a high, grating sound.

"Well, sir, I think you might be very much interested in seeing some of the items I have here."

"No, boy. I wouldn't be interested in nothing you've got there."

"Well, is there anyone at home who might be?"

"Don't ask me." The old man looked less amused as his mouth turned down in two separate folds. "I don't know if they're home in that damned house or if they want anything or not. I'm just the father of one of the people that live there. Don't expect me to know anything."

John waited on the walk while the old man stared at the ground, brooding. Then his expression changed, and he squinted up at John. "But if I was you," he said, "I wouldn't waste my time with them, home or not." John picked up his suitcase and walked toward the street. The old man laughed again.

"Boy, you're not going to be an executive if you don't try no harder than that."

The old man was still laughing as John turned into the next yard and knocked on the front door.

A woman wearing a blue satin housecoat opened the door and told John to come right in. He followed her into a living room filled with precisely arranged, highly polished furniture, and sat down on a curve-legged chair that seemed too fragile to hold him. Little wall shelves were suspended around the room, crowded with glass ornaments and miniature vases filled with artificial flowers.

The woman sat down across from John. She was about forty, and her face was beginning to sag behind a little-girl prettiness. Her skin was covered with cream and powder that, combined, made her appear to be layered in white plaster. The housecoat curved snugly around her body and was shining so that John had the giddy impression she might be plaster all over.

"Well, I guess I'd just as well show you everything," John said when she had settled herself on the divan.

"Yes, do," the woman answered. "I want to see everything." John opened the case, then glanced up and noticed that the woman was looking at him very intently.

"I'm sorry," she said, when she saw that he was watching her. "I'm sorry that I don't seem to be paying attention to your things. I was just wondering if you were thirsty. It's awfully warm out today."

"No, ma'am, I'm not thirsty."

"Oh, you must be. I'll run out and fix you something."

"No, thank you. I'm not thirsty," John repeated, feeling helpless.

"Don't you say another word," the woman said, shaking her finger at him. "It won't take a minute." She got up then and slowly left the room, walking deliberately as though she needed to concentrate on what she was doing.

John could hear her moving around in the kitchen. He could not relax in the fragile chair. Everything in the room was so polished and brittle-looking that he was sure something would shatter if he moved too much.

The woman returned and, quietly slipping behind John's chair, she reached over his shoulder to hand him the drink. "It's more or less lemonade," she said. "Just a teeny bit of gin to give it flavor. Lemonade's so tasteless by itself."

The heavy flower scent of her perfume mingled with the gin, and he tightened against the small, queasy lurch in his stomach. "Thank you. I really didn't need anything."

"Well, now, let's see what we've got here." She moved back to the divan, but instead of sitting down, she took a silk cushion from the end and dropped it to the floor by John's feet. She sat on the cushion and began to examine the paper products. "You're rather young to be working already."

"Yes, ma'am. Have you seen our oil-treated furniture dusters?"

"No. No, I haven't." She smiled up at him as though he'd said something delightfully naughty.

John set his drink on the glass-topped table beside his chair and leaned down to find the furniture duster. He felt the woman's warm hands brushing lightly against his face. The upper part of her body was pressed against one of his knees, and he was surprised at the softness of what had looked so glass-hard and brittle. Then the woman was kissing him in a way that he had not known you could be kissed. A flood of warmth rushed from his head down to his knees. He strained away. The woman held firmly to his neck now, her eyebrows squeezed together, her jaws hollow, and her lips protruding. John pushed her away and stood up, afraid that he was going to be sick in the center of the well-waxed floor. He closed the suitcase and walked weak-kneed to the front door. The woman hurried up beside him as he fumbled the latch. "Don't leave," she said, her smooth forehead broken into three lines of wrinkles. "Don't be afraid of me."

"I've got to go, madam," John said as he opened the door. He wanted very much to get outside, and at the same time he wanted to be back in the spindly chair feeling as weak and helpless as he had felt before. He ran down the porch steps and walked rapidly for a block without looking back toward the house.

It was two o'clock. He sat on his suitcase beneath one of the poplar trees to wait for Mr. Curtis. While he waited, his mind moving over all that had happened in the past hour, it occurred to him for the first time that he was never going to be a boy again. He would have to go on being a man now until he died. He rubbed his face with his handkerchief and began to feel as tired as he had ever felt.

THOMAS F. WILLIAMS lives in Locust Grove, Virginia. He is a graduate of Southern Illinois University and had an additional year of study at the National University of Mexico. He served as officer-in-charge of a landing craft during World War II. While he has had many types of employment, his most significant work began in 1956 when he became a public information specialist with the U.S. Department of Health, Education, and Welfare and later with the Environmental Protection Agency, from which he retired in 1980. He has been credited with having played a key role in bringing public and Congressional attention to the importance of environmental issues.

JOE LUNIEVICZ

Stuffed

Jamie Wyeth.
Coast Guard Anchor.
Watercolor on paper,
1982. Farnsworth Art
Museum, Rockland,
Maine.

CHANGE DOESN T COME EASY TO ME, I'll admit. Like the time channel seven canceled the four-thirty movie and put on another talk show with a Mike Douglas look-a-like. Not that I don't enjoy the talk shows. It's just that I was used to the timing; four-thirty, channel seven, and that music from *Spartacus*. It helped me remember who I was and where I was at, like a pointer on one of those maps at the mall saying, "You are here."

It was the last week in October, and I was getting ready to go down to The Roost. I go every Monday night during the season to catch the football games, have a few beers, and watch the kids neck in the corner booths during the commercials. This is Brooklyn, you know. They haven't gotten into that body slamming crap I've heard about in Manhattan. Kids still know how to touch each other here—like human beings. Since I was seventeen, kids have done that at bars on Seventh Avenue, though when I was seventeen, I was one of them in the booths rather than one of them watching like I do now. I guess I'm kind of a voyeur. I don't think it hurts anyone though, or I'd stop doing it.

October is an important month to me, being all of seventy-eight years of age, and I was thinking on that before I left the house that evening. That and the fact that the four-thirty movie wasn't around anymore had been worrying at my mind. At my age you get used to certain things happening in certain ways. Metamucil and five different kinds of pills in the morning. I don't even know their names—just their colors and the fact that one of them says "Do not take with alcoholic beverages." There are two small white ones the size of hearing aide batteries, a big yellow one from Squib that sticks in my throat when I try to swallow it, and two light green ones that look like navy peas. Beth used to know them all by name—arrange them for us at night sitting at the kitchen table so we'd have them ready in the morning. She'd put them in two paper napkins folded over at the corners so they looked like kites.

I usually have some bran too, to even out the Metamucil—internally I mean. Although sometimes, I say what the hell and have a few chocolate donuts instead. You tell me. How many years is it going to take off of my life, and at this point does it really matter?

You mess things up if you don't follow the pattern of things. My wife, God rest her soul, she died five years ago of cancer. They took off both her breasts before she went, and she had beautiful breasts. That was before they did lumpectomies. It was a 'cut and mutilate before it's too late' job. I used to rhyme that to myself so much, it became like a jingle from a commercial I couldn't get out of my head. It didn't matter anyway. They were just words. It spread fast and took her early.

I remember the falsies she wore always slipped down on her. We went to dinner with some friends one time, and I remember saying to her, "Beth your third base is sliding in to home," because that's just what the right side was doing. She lost her hair too. I used to comb it for her, until it started to come out in patches.

I guess the hardest part about deciding to decide to change is that you really don't want to change to begin with. Take me for instance. At my age I've come to terms with it. I can be like a rock in a river bed; at least that's what my daughter tells me. And I'll tell you some things just shouldn't change, like a good Louis Lamour novel. That guy can write. You come to expect certain things in his books, and he always delivers. That's consistency. You read his pages, and you get your due. No forgetting where your keys are, or your boxers, or your wallet, and no morning ghosts between his covers.

Monday evening before I left the house, I went through a dresser drawer I usually use for underwear storage, looking for my backup bottle of Old Spice, when I found Beth's old falsies. They were staring up at me—two dark mounds peeking out from behind a pair of worn plaid boxers. I closed the drawer quickly and grabbed my walking stick, which I still have from WWII. Instead of walking into The Roost, I stopped in front of it and looked inside from the window. There was a young couple in the far booth necking. I could swear I saw a hand cup a sweatered breast, and I remembered the falsies in the drawer staring up at me like two dark orbs. I waved at my friends inside, hunched over the bar, beer mugs in hands, eyes glazed over, watching the game on the television like a couple of stuffed game birds on a trophy shelf. I waved to them slowly because I was still seeing those two dark orbs and the hand on the sweater breast. I wished they'd go away, and when they did, I remembered seeing my grandson give my daughter the finger when she told him he couldn't stay the night with his own grandfather "cause he was a drunk," after she turned her back to give me that evil eye of hers. I don't know who she learned that from. It's so damned disrespectful.

I guess I didn't see the boys at the bar anymore. I was seeing sweater breasts and my grandson's middle finger and something else I guess, because I shot Big Eddie Cosnowsky the bird, with him looking me right in the eyes from between the "o"s in the Coors sign. I thought he was watching the game, but he spit up his beer all over himself so I guess he was watching me. Lenny the bartender spilled the beer he was carrying over to Eddie's drinking partner, Joe Stuborov. It landed on Joe's lap. The couple in the corner that was necking saw the whole thing and started to laugh. And me I finally wasn't seeing sweater breasts and dark orbs, so I flipped them all a second-handed one. Big Ed and Joey began to curse. I could see the foam starting on their lips like a couple of rabid animals. They waved their fists at me and hit each other in the arm in the process, but I didn't care. I felt possibility surround me. I stood there laughing. There was bright light in my head, and all my memories seemed clear, like a road map of my life up to this point.

"You are here," it said, and the arrow was red neon like the Coors sign, and it flashed on and off like it was alarming everyone to an emergency situation. All I could think of was I wished Beth was here so she could see it hadn't all been a waste. That I'd been somewhere. That I still had someplace to go. So, I took the moment and did what I thought I couldn't do. I made a change.

I left them there, glued to their stools like arm-waving, dust-covered taxiderms. I walked down the street quickly, so I wouldn't change my mind, past the new Austin drug store, where there used to be an old five and dime, and then the Methodist church. I always duck my head passing there out of respect. Beth used to go there every Sunday. Pray for my soul, she used to say. Pray for my soul. Maybe she should have prayed for her own. Maybe she would've lasted a little longer, and I would've had something more than two dark orbs staring up at me from an underwear drawer to hold on to. Maybe I would've had more than that four-thirty movie music to remind me who I was and where I was at. I passed the Methodist and headed towards Fedderman's Drug Store—only Fedderman's isn't there anymore either. Now it's Emerson's Bar and Grill.

I walked inside after catching my breath and took a bar stool by the big screen television. I ordered a beer. The Giants were playing the Eagles on channel two. There wasn't a single old man in the place. There was a young bartender who didn't know me, watching the game, ignoring me. Well he ignored me only until I rapped my stick across the bar top a few times and broke a glass that just happened to get in my way. Beth always said I had a temper when I was at the trough. He drew me a tap fast, and I tasted the gold. I looked over at the corner table and saw a couple there necking. The Giants scored a touchdown on the big screen, and the couple came up for air long enough to get a new grip on each other. The lip lock was pretty fierce. I never was any good at that kind of stuff. Beth always had to guide me. "You're too rough," she'd say. "Pucker more," she'd say.

Things do change, though.

I looked around and realized I wasn't at The Roost. The walls weren't paneled, and Big Ed and Joey were nowhere in sight. I didn't know the bartender. Sometimes things just don't make sense to me. It's happened before. It's like I've got it right in the palm of my hand, and when I go to close my fingers around it, it's gone.

I felt someone tap me on the shoulder, and I thought I heard Beth's voice from behind me say, "Excuse me, is this seat taken?" Only it wasn't Beth. You see Beth's been gone for over five years now. Five years and counting. I'm as sure of it as I am of that music from *Spartacus* announcing the return of the four-thirty movie.

JOE LUNIEVICZ has had literary fiction published in both national and regional publications, including *Smoke, Aberrations, 96INC., Amelia, Dragon Magazine,* and *Another Chicago Magazine.* His nonfiction has appeared in *Body Positive* and *Rugby* (where he wrote the "Zen Rugger" column). He is also a playwright and lives in New York City.

DON KISSIL

Lessons Learned from a Sanitized America

THE OLDER I GET, THE MORE I REALIZE that my education did not end
in the too many classes I had sat in or slept through. Every day I comprehend more of the subtle differences between learning and education, between intellect and intelligence, and sometimes I even get an
inkling of understanding of the biblical reference to Solomon's wisdom (in Hebrew called "Chochma") as opposed to the "knowledge
from one's own experience" that the Quaker, George Fox, talked
about. Let me tell you of some "experience" lessons that taught me
much, and they all occurred long after I left school.

I collected the young Japanese social scientist at Newark
International Airport in the chill of a late November afternoon. Her
twelve hours in the turbulent air had extracted its toll. I needn't have
worried about the language problem. Akiko's face told all. A cup of
coffee, cream and sugar, in the airport bar brought a bit of color back
to her lips, as we two virtual strangers began to interact.

No, she'd never been to our East Coast before. Her only
American experience had been a California trip with her parents
when she was twelve. Yes, she'd like to see the skyline of New York as
the sun was setting. Yes, she too was from a big city, Tokyo, but New
York City always held some kind of magic for her.

Magic eh! Interesting, perhaps there was a poet's soul caught in
that sociologist body. So with less regard for language and cultural
differences and a greater concern to try to save the afternoon light,
we snaked through the airport parking lot and on to Jersey City.

Mary Cassatt.
The Letter.
Drypoint and aquatint,
from three plates, in
blue, tan/fawn,
pink/rose, brown, green,
black, light brown/dark
yellow, and a touch of
red c.l. in the margin, on
off-white laid paper,
34.5×21.1 cm.,
1890–1891.
The Art Institute
of Chicago. Mr. and Mrs.
Martin A. Ryerson
Collection.

"There we'd find the best view of the New York skyline from the Hudson River waterfront. Also there you may experience the wizardry of the Liberty Science Center and the serenity of Liberty State Park during autumn. A Japanese friend told me that your name, Akiko, means autumn in English, so I thought you might be in your element there." That last bit was my feeble attempt at the concept of Japanese balance.

The cold was brutal for that time of year, as the warmed, once crisp air belched from the mouths of the few pedestrians we passed. Their air clouds reminded me of the smokestacks from Jersey City's many industrial parks.

During the ride I tried to explain, often with frustration, several English words and concepts I thought she might find difficult. Words and phrases like old brownstones that had become *yuppified* or *gentrified*, and the general *urban blight* of old houses juxtaposed to abandoned rusted cars.

Could this young woman, accustomed to the homogeneity of the Japanese population, really understand our American heterogeneity? Could she comprehend our multicultural and multiracial urban populations, many of whom were illegal or certainly undocumented, but of necessity supply a cheap labor force to almost every American City?

She might understand our faux glitter and glitz, given the unprecedented cyclical changes of the Japanese economy in the past quarter century. With the Internet and E-commerce turning both our nations into speed freaks, she might understand why most of our super malls, hypermarkets, and shopping centers were now functionally bankrupt and silently waiting to collapse, while our fast-food joints and entry-level service jobs have, however, burgeoned.

Could the expressionless expressions on the faces we saw through our car windows as we crossed town convey any meaning to her? They were the people that few Japanese, and indeed far too few Americans, ever saw. As we drove I wondered if we have sanitized our America and if our media manipulators have exported that vision worldwide. I thought that too many Americans (and perhaps even myself) continue to drink from that sanitized cup.

THE MAGNIFICENT SUNSET painted the Manhattan skyline as so many Pre-Colombian temples growing out of the jungle. Looking west, Akiko said: "The color of the sky above your Jersey City now takes on that purple hue we Japanese understand comes from the ash in the air when one of our volcanoes erupt." I wondered if our industrial pollution was anything like volcanic ash.

As the evening chill grew more intense, we both agreed to return to reality. Our destination was my home in the suburbs, and Akiko asked how long it would take us to arrive there. Remembering her twelve-hour air vigil, I said we'd be there in about half an hour. She smiled and said: "The drive from our Norita Airport in Tokyo to our suburbs would take at least two hours. And I thought your eastern cities would show more 'urban blight' and sprawl than ours!" I smiled that she had already integrated one of our American expressions into her vocabulary.

MAYBE IT WAS THE WARMTH OF THE CAR, or perhaps the unlighted highway darkness, broken only by the red taillights of high-drive traffic leaving Center City for our burbs, but this part of the trip allowed our muses to return. She began to notice the cars whizzing past us and said: "Sooo many BMWs, Mercedes, and Porsches here. They are certainly different than those cars we saw earlier in your Jersey City."

I countered with another smile and said, "These cars are above the city. I mean, literally they are on that part of the New Jersey Turnpike that is elevated above Jersey City, Bayonne, and Newark. And these cars are painted in only one color. That color is either New or Clean. Those down below are more often multicolored like dirt, rust, rot and re-paint."

Her quizzical look did not last long, and coyly she responded: "Do you think bald, as in tires, is a color also?" I chuckled with a growing confidence that no matter where her work here would take her, she would do a grand job of it.

At our home, for the short while she was with us, Akiko almost at once became the jovial college undergraduate not much different than our own kids were at her age. Up to that time our knowledge of Japanese culture was limited to old Kurosawa movies featuring lots of Samurai grunting, groaning, and swordplay, and an occasional sushi bar. So the first thing Akiko introduced us to was the film-maker, Juso Itami and his very funny spoof of the spaghetti western called "Tampopo." That video and several others Itami produced taught me that the Japanese could, in fact laugh at themselves. So maybe that was the first lesson I learned—what you see ain't necessarily what you get. Then we spent several hours of hilarious lessons on the proper way to execute the correct Japanese bow and how to sit in that awful Asian position with your feet tucked under your butt with the blood circulation to your legs tournequetted.

Yes, we learned a lot from Akiko. But let me give you some background before I continue.

A LONG-TIME MEMBER OF OUR QUAKER MEETING here in New Jersey had relocated back to his birthplace in Japan to teach sociology at a Japanese University. One of his young undergraduate students designed a research project to be done in the United States and sought his help. That student was Akiko, and she was not a Quaker. Our old Friend wrote to me and described her research proposal. I was so fascinated with it that I offered her my home and any services I could, to facilitate her project.

Akiko's protocol involved interviewing ten American conscientious objectors to war. She would ask them several open-ended questions that would encourage them to recall their history and motivation for why they chose to take that action. As several older members of our Quaker Meeting had been COs, my job would be to get them together with Akiko for her to interview them.

When she'd completed her interviews, my curiosity overcame my hesitation, and I asked her about some of her results. Her first few questions dealt with the nuts and bolts of why, how, when, and where they took that action. The next few dealt with the consequences they faced for their decision. Her last question brought forth the most soul-searching reflections. It was a stunner! She asked her interviewees:

> You know, of course, that during the WWII in Japan, there was a small but active pacifist community. But our government would not permit conscientious objection to war. If you applied for that, you were summarily executed by the state, with no trial. Now, if the same situation occurred here in the U. S., would you still register as a CO?

Akiko said the answers to this question were the most interesting and unexpected. She would not elaborate in order, she said, to permit her to maintain the confidentiality she needed.

"But how did you feel about their answers to that last question?" I asked.

Akiko answered in a more serious tone than she'd ever exhibited before. She said: "I'm doing research, collecting data; it would not be proper for me to editorialize or to make judgments at this time. Maybe I'll tell you my feelings after my research is completed."

Naively, when I tried to push, she answered: "Some men, after a long silence, simply did not answer. Others spoke, albeit hesitantly, but . . ."

And here she paused, perhaps searching for the best words to use. "They seemed to answer mostly from their head not from their heart."

When I heard this my mind drifted back to when I draft counseled during the Vietnam War. Some questions the Draft Board would put before an interviewee, applying for CO status, simply should not be answered. They were intended to trap you into a no-win situation, so that CO status could more easily be denied.

My thoughts spun off in several different directions. I thought about how times had changed after all these years, but had they really? I thought about the number of wars that had passed since WW II, and how many of our young American men had evolved in their concept of conscientious objection to war.

A founding member of our Quaker Meeting drove an ambulance as a CO as long ago as WW I. Another, a doctor, spent a year in Federal prison for making that choice during WW II, while others in our Meeting thought "that war was different." And now with the arrival of our present day "political correctness," much of our American thinking about war and pacifism had changed, too. I remembered how some time ago our U.S. Supreme Court issued a ruling saying you could be a CO even without having a particular religious conviction. And while my Quaker thinking still allowed me to question authority as I continued to learn, I'd not given up on my pacifist beliefs.

But I wondered how our American thinking on the issue of conscientious objection to war might translate to other nations. I thought about all the Balkanized states of the former Yugoslavia, while ethnic cleansing was taking place. I pondered the righteousness of the Palestinian versus the Israeli positions, while bombs fell on the Lebanese and pipe bomb explosions killed other Middle East peoples. The attempts at settlement of the "troubles" in Ireland, while children were being blown up, continuously shouted at me from the TV.

The still small voices for nonviolent resolutions to conflict remain, but unfortunately few seem to hear those voices over the din of cries for war. The recent war in Chiapas, Mexico, and the decades of ongoing war against the Mayan Indians of Guatemala have all but suppressed the voices for peace. Are they now all silenced?

Perhaps those who choose to drink from the sanitized cup of media spins or walk in the light of political correctness may sleep through the next few decades of change. But, at the risk of sounding too much like a sixties hippy, I do think that change is blowing in the wind.

Akiko was with us only a few days before she left for San Francisco to interview several more COs there. I never heard from her again, and I was left to ponder just what I had learned from this late-in-life educational experience. Perhaps her research will make Asia the agent for peaceful change. Maybe it will be the poet-sociologist-humanitarian in all of us who will be the hands of God to bring peace.

DON KISSIL, who was born sixty-seven years ago in The Bronx, now lives in New Jersey. A licensed pharmacist by academic training, he has worked as research scientist, medical writer, ad copywriter, and for more than thirty years wrote as a freelancer. He has also edited a bluegrass music magazine, written and published non-fiction in *Medicine,* in *Music,* and in *Travel & Birding,* and has been translated into several languages. Today he writes fiction for children, including several illustrated picture books on the Mayans and their mythology.

LORRAINE SANDO

When Spirit Moves

FIVE DAYS BEFORE JACK'S DEATH, I HAD A DREAM. I saw a white dove flying. It had flown out of our house. I was deeply concerned; it belonged in the house. I opened the door, and the dove returned. Next, I was with a woman going through things, pieces of used fabric and clothing. They kept coming out of suitcases and the top of the bed and from under the bed. It was overwhelming. When I awakened, I knew the white dove symbolized peace, and I knew it was a messenger of death. Carl Jung calls the bird a symbol of transcendence. He speaks also of the shaman, whose power resides in his supposed ability to leave his body and fly about the universe as a bird. I believe the white dove symbolizes Jack's leaving via death and the reentry of the holy spirit.

On Friday, it happened. I rushed Jack to the hospital late in the evening. From the emergency room, it was decided to admit him to

Lorraine Sando.
Fire Tree.
Acrylic, 2000.

the hospital. When the doctors left to find him a room, he asked me to help him to sit up. He was so uncomfortable. I held him briefly in sitting position before he fell backward on the cold gurney. His eyes rolled back in his head, and somehow I knew he was dead. I tugged at his heavy body to keep him on the narrow bed and rushed out in the hall for help. The heroic efforts that I watched from the rear of the room need not have been. I later discovered the directive to physicians we'd written a decade earlier could have prevented the shocks that Jack's body endured. With each shock, his body leaped up off the table. The physician came to me. I said, "He wants to go; let him go." Then his heart started to beat tentatively, and he left me for the Intensive Care Unit. The doctor held me silently. My immobile body was in crisis mode. My self had gone deep inside.

We went into Jack's room and spent two hours there. My five-year-old grandson, Devin, touched Grampa, talked with him, asked questions. My twelve-year-old granddaughter, Kayla, stood beside her mother with tears flowing down her cheeks. We said our good-byes, our tributes, our rememberings as we embraced his body. My two oldest sons and Barbara stood by in deep sorrow, touching his spirit with their hearts, supporting us in our sorrow.

For me there followed two months of shock. Blindly functioning, my mind had left my body. I moved through my days and duties; my eyes were dry. My sleep was deep and dreamless. Then September came, and the insomnia settled in, an unwelcome visitor. It went on for seven months, my affair with the stealthful sleep robber. Oh, I always got the first two hours of the night. The rest was sleepless.

Before Jack died, I knew I'd always have my work and my friends. I felt more whole and healthier than I'd ever experienced. The sharp explosive sword of death shattered me. My life as two was gone. I had to rebuild from ashes and small pieces—an ominous task. My body went through the movements of living, reminding myself to be super-alert when driving my car. My concentration wandered between past, present, and future. My mind flitted from one picture to another like a robin searching in vain for nourishment.

Where had my deep spirituality gone? Where was God anyway—was there really a God?—my thinking shocked me. I remember that when Jung was asked, "Do you believe in God?" he hesitated a long time and finally said in a deliberate hushed voice—"I don't believe—I know." I knew too. But where was God now? I felt abandoned by a God who I deeply trusted.

That summer found me teaching, consulting with churches, carrying on with a reduced private-practice case load, functioning well behind a fragile fleshy shell. And then September came, and I couldn't delude myself any longer. The heavy dark cloud of grief settled over me as insomnia and hip pain became unwanted guests. Everyone said, when you can't sleep, get up and do something, don't just lie in wait for morning. But I stayed in my warm bed. It was comforting. Jack's essence was there. I tried talking with him. I thought I felt his presence, but I heard nothing. Memories of the three sons conceived in this bed, the wonderful times of making love, the bedtime conversations when the night created a warm soft time of close secrets that could not easily be shared in the light of day. Books became sleep partners in our bed as we drifted off to sleep. His books usually slipped to the floor, and his glasses drooped off his nose. I would reach over him to turn out the lamp and remove his glasses. He always went to sleep first.

I envied his ability to leave the day behind and easily slide into darkness. He did that on that emergency room table, slipped into his new life without telling me goodbye, in words that is, although, when I was writing his eulogy, Jack shut down my computer a couple of times, letting me know he was close.

He had always been supportive of my work, my church, our family, and me. His death created a huge chasm. My perception of myself dove deeply into despair and anxiety. How was I to manage everything on my own?

We were partners and each doing what we loved. I never did taxes or finances. I never fixed broken refrigerators, the vacuum, the lights, and I never programmed the TVs, VCRs, or the telephones and computers. Jack was an electrical engineer—he could fix anything. I didn't want to learn to do these things, and for a long time I wouldn't try. My mind couldn't focus on directions, books, nor could I remember what I read for more than five minutes. Irrational thinking such as fears of being a bag lady, fears of getting a serious illness, inability to focus or concentrate, distractibility, a seriously damaged self-esteem were the new bed partners. Others said you must reduce your stress. I didn't know how. Despite all of my therapeutic skills, I couldn't access them for myself.

NOW, MANY MONTHS LATER, having extricated some truths from my bed of despair, I celebrate myself. Here's what I did:

I reached out to friends.

I did not wait for them to call.

I asked for help over and over and over again.

I began to develop neighborhood friends.

I went to two grief groups.

I continued seeing a clinical nutritionist and have been able to
    keep my immune system healthy during this dangerous time
    of grief.

I planned something to get me out of the house daily.

I continued my three-hour-a-week painting sessions.

The paintings were done just before Jack died and in the months
following his death. My painting feeds my spirit. I meet and play with
God here and always through the darkest paintings, darkest nights
of my soul, the light of hope burns strongly awaiting my return into
the fullness of light. I painted myself through my fears and sorrow
and began a new love affair with the sensual oil colors on my palette,
the textures made by wax additions, oil bars, and mixed media.

The first nine months were dark, lonely, filled with anxiety and
fear. It was a kind of hell I'd never known before. Then my paintings
of the "Fire Tree" and "Tree of Life" emerged, and my faith broke
through to consciousness. And there was the "Where the Two Worlds
Touch" from the wonderful Rumi poem translated by Coleman
Barks.

The breeze at dawn has secrets to tell, Don't go back to Sleep
You must ask for what you really want, Don't go back to Sleep

People are traveling back and forth across the threshold where
    the two Worlds touch.
The door is round and open
Don't go back to sleep.

A new friend offered me this poem in the height of my insomnia. One day in July near the anniversary of Jack's death, I decided to
memorize it. After this anniversary, I painted the paintings. I'm now
consciously connecting with my beloved; tears now come easily; they
are tears of joy as well as sadness that he isn't here to watch his
beloved grandchildren grow up. Sometimes birds speak to me of his
presence. On the anniversary of his death, a quail came close to my
glass patio door and stood silently gazing into my eyes. Yesterday
morning while lying in my hammock on my patio, little six-year-old
Devin came to join me. We cuddled up to keep warm on this second
day of September. Then I heard again the bird call that I knew sig-
naled a communication from the other world, and I knew Jack was
present. I talked to Devin about it. He said, "Gramma, I don't know
about that." I said, "Devin, that is just fine. It's very, very important
that you question everything."

My high self-esteem has returned and is much stronger. I have a
tremendously renewed spirited spirituality. And much more. The
most priceless prize I won from my pathway through grief is my sol-

id ability to intuit, to trust and believe in the abundance that is constantly available to me.

The other day I was going through pictures and memorabilia
and listening to the wonderful song by Nat King Cole *Unforgettable*
that was played at the memorial service, when a communication
came. My organizational helper and I were standing in the kitchen,
Unforgettable was playing, and we both heard a knock on the door. I
went to the door, and no one was there. I said to her, "That was Jack."

LORRAINE SANDO is an artist, psychotherapist, consultant, trainer, and
writer. She loves her work and sees her life as a wonderful journey in
process. She joined the Swedenborgian Church in 1964 and since then has
served on many of its local and national boards and committees. She says
"My job on this earth is to be of use and make this world a better place for
all those who follow." She lives in Seattle, surrounded by her three sons and
their families and many friends.

Offerings

Winter morning arrives
Expectant as a blank page,
An envelope waiting to be filled.
I have only a few words to offer.

All week a stray cat
Stepping like jazz piano
Has come into the yard
Sniffing for food.

Out of nowhere his hunger
Makes room for me.
I watch him return to my offerings,
Both of us dreaming

The easy flight of birds.
In the cold months, in the
Early darkness things grow tender,
Amplified by the sharp tick of the clock.

If it were a guest, I would ask it to leave.
Ellis and Christian, blonde and dark-eyed
As mythical children,
Beg me to read to them.

I pull other worlds from the shelf
And soon their questions
Demand a detour.
How can I describe

That which is in constant transformation,
Things like pleasure and desire
That are never certain,
But learned forever.

Nominated twice for the *Pushcart Prize*, CORRINE DE WINTER's poetry, fiction, essays, and interviews have appeared in *The New York Quarterly, Imago, Phoebe, Plainsongs, Yankee, Sacred Journey, Interim, The Lucid Stone, Fate, Press, Sulphur River Literary Review, Modern Poetry, The Lyric, Atom Mind, The Writer, The Lyric,* and over 600 other publications.

WANDA LUTTRELL

A Search for Meaning

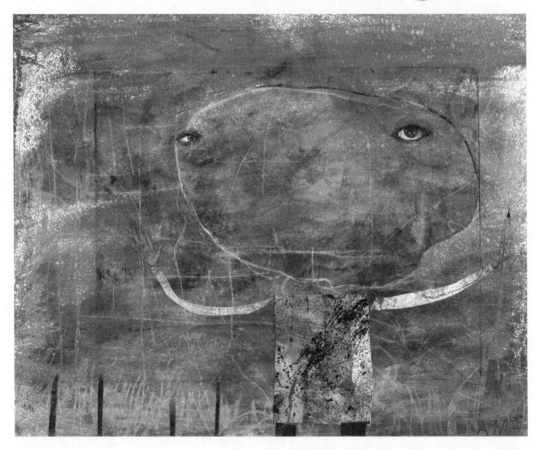

Alan Magee.
Childhood and History.
Monotype collage, 1989.

HELEN GRACE NODDED AND SMILED in response to a last chorus of "Goodbye!" "See you next year!" as the stragglers juggled books, long-lost sweaters, and report cards in their rush to catch buses.

She hadn't had the heart to tell them. Most of them, though, would be fifth-graders when school opened next fall, with a new teacher and exciting new worlds to conquer. The fact that their fourth-grade teacher had retired would trouble them little.

Exhausted, she sank down in the chair behind the oak desk in front of the blackboard. This room in the original wing of Bald Knob Elementary had been assigned to her that first year when she had come fresh out of teachers' college.

Nine months of each of the past thirty-five years, she had spent here. Fourth-graders had come and gone. Styles, customs, and social standards had changed, but she had seen to it that Miss Grace's fourth grade remained constant, a steady anchor in a shifting world.

She opened the shallow center drawer and sorted things she would take home from those she would leave for her replacement. That done, she turned to the books on the right corner of the desk, placing in one pile to remain behind, the dictionary, the teacher's editions of current textbooks, the character-building *Singing Wheels* she had talked the central office into letting her continue to use after the more modern reading texts had been issued.

Helen smiled, remembering Tommy Baker's comment last fall when he had come back to tell her he was enrolled in seminary.

Tommy will make a wonderful preacher, she thought. Then she blushed, remembering his next words. "You're beautiful, Miss Grace," he had said, bending down to kiss her on the cheek.

She put up one hand to touch the spot. Beautiful! she thought. What nonsense! She had never been beautiful, and now she was an old, gray-haired lady with sun-wrinkles and age-spots! Of course, she knew Tommy had been referring to her inner qualities. Only her dear mother ever had thought she was outwardly beautiful.

She sighed. Papa had died when she was a teenager, and his memory was like a faded photograph, but even after fifteen years she still missed Mama. There's no one left who thinks I'm beautiful, she thought, knowing that she had come to terms with her lack of physical beauty long ago. And, despite her appreciation of the classics, she knew that hers was an ordinary mind.

"I'm a good fourth-grade teacher," she said aloud, surveying the handiwork of her students—the pictures and writings secured by snap clothespins to strings stretched along three walls, the rock collection on the back bookcase, the pioneer fort made of popsicle sticks, scraps of material and Elmer's glue.

She was going to miss this room, the daily routines, the students. Her children, she thought. So many boys and girls—some of them grown now with children, and even grandchildren of their own—whose lives had been entwined with hers for a time.

Would the ripples of everyday school life close over her space without a sign that Helen Grace ever had filled it? That's the way it had been last year when Selma Young retired after twenty-eight years of teaching second grade. No one seemed to miss her now, except Helen. But, to whom would the teachers, the clerical staff, even some of the parents, go for help when she was gone? Who would stay after school to help Clayton Coubert with his reading or help Allie Shelton hem up her hand-me-downs?

Helen often had felt that this small school was a mission field to which she had been called thirty-five years ago. Was she running out on her duty by retiring? She wouldn't be sixty until November. Lately though, she simply lacked the energy to cope with some of the home situations, the degradation of television shows and movies, and the insidious drugs and alcohol that reached greedily for even her fourth-graders.

She glanced around the room, calculating what remained to be done before she closed it up for the summer. But it wasn't just for the summer. This room had been her life! She entered it each morning with a feeling of excitement, and left it almost every evening with a sense of satisfaction. Now, she faced endless days of sameness.

Helen became aware of the deep silence around her. Was she the last one in the building again? The custodian was a patient man, but he liked to get things wrapped up early on Fridays and especially on the last day of school.

She peered into the hallway and saw the principal's office door was open, as it often was after hours. Helen had loved Ned Mason dearly, but she had to admit that after that first year of adjustment following his death, Almada Templeton had made the school run like a well-oiled machine.

Mrs. Templeton had asked her to call her Almada, but, no matter that she was ten years Helen's junior, she simply couldn't do it. The first name familiarity seemed disrespectful to her. The best she could do was to address the principal as "Mrs. T."

Ned Mason had urged Helen to go into administration herself. "You practically wrote the county's elementary teaching guide, Helen. You'd make an excellent supervisor of elementary instruction," he'd said several times. Then he had warned, "Administration is the only way you'll ever make any money in the education profession."

But she hadn't gone into teaching to make money. For her, teaching was a calling, one that had been clear from the time she was a little girl playing school with her dolls. No, she hadn't made a lot of money, but she didn't need a lot.

She recalled the lean days of her college years when she had worked after classes and between semesters to earn tuition. Now, though, she had most of the money from the sale of the farm laid by, and she had kept the house and garden, so she had no mortgage or rent payments. With her retirement, she could continue to live comfortably.

I am not an administrator, she thought. *I am a good teacher. Mrs. T. is a good administrator. And we are providing the boys and girls of this community an education equal to any in the Commonwealth, maybe even in the nation. The world?* she thought, then laughed aloud at her boastfulness. "What are you laughing about here at 4 PM on the last day of school?" a familiar husky voice asked from the doorway.

"Oh, Mrs. T," Helen answered, flushing, "I was just thinking that Bald Knob Elementary is as good as any school in the Commonwealth, and . . ."

"That's not funny, Helen. That's the truth!!" the principal interrupted, with a grin that widened her generous mouth and sparkled in her blue eyes.

"But then I expanded that to the nation, and finally my pride took on the whole world!" Helen admitted. She laughed again, and the principal joined her.

"But I'm inclined to agree with your pride," Almada Templeton said. "You know, Helen, those awards for excellence we've received recently to a large degree have been your awards."

"Why, Mrs. T!" She swallowed her embarrassment. "I've only done my job," she finished firmly.

The principal shook her head. "Your influence has done more than you'll ever know to get new teachers started off on the right foot and to encourage the experienced ones to strive for excellence. I wish we had a dozen more just like you!"

Helen realized that the principal had moved closer, and she looked up into frank blue eyes studying her as though she were making one last evaluation.

"You're a jewel, Helen Grace," she said huskily, giving Helen's shoulder a firm squeeze. "I don't know what I'll ever do without you!" And she was gone.

Deliberately, she turned her thoughts to clearing the room of the things that had made it hers. She was packing the last box, wondering how she would get the heavy books and plants to her car, when she felt someone watching her.

"Why, Clayton, did you forget something?" she asked the boy in the doorway. He lived just beyond her house and often walked home with her after they finished his after-school remedial reading.

"No, Ma'am." For a moment, he stared at the toes of his torn tennis shoes, then his dark eyes met hers. "I didn't look at my report card 'till I got home, thinking for sure I'd failed. Then I seen . . . uh . . . saw that you'd passed me!"

"You've improved a great deal this last semester, Clayton. I think you're ready for fifth grade."

The boy shook his head. "I don't think I can do them fractions and long divisions, Miz Grace. And I still need help with my tronics."

"Phonics," Helen corrected absently, her mind busy with a new idea. "I'll be glad to continue helping you, Clayton," she offered, "if you'll come by my house in the evenings after school." She waved away the protest she saw his fierce pride constructing. "You can pay me in advance by carrying some things to my car."

Relief spread over his face. "Oh, Miz Grace, I'll do anything you need—mow grass, cut wood, anything. If you'll help me, I think maybe I can handle fifth grade!"

After Clayton had carried her things to the car and disappeared down the road, Helen stood behind her desk for the last time. Except for the rows of empty desks, the room was practically bare now. Only the district-issued pictures of historic shrines and the maps and charts the PTA had bought remained on the walls. The room was no longer hers. It was time to go.

"Have you got a minute, Helen?"

She knew, without looking up, that the voice belonged to Charlotte Newby, a teacher just out of college who had taken Selma Young's second grade last fall. Charlotte was by no means Helen's favorite. Her clothes were a bit too tight, and she had an annoying way of calling her elders by their first names without invitation.

To be fair, though, Helen knew that her resentment was mostly because she had replaced her dear colleague, and because Charlotte had acknowledged their introduction with an amused glance that took in Helen's homemade dress and sensible shoes, and dismissed her as hopelessly old-fashioned.

Well, I am old-fashioned, Helen thought. She didn't envy Charlotte! In fact, sometimes she felt a little sorry for her. Despite her busy social life, she seemed lonely.

"Come in and sit down, Charlotte," she invited reluctantly, and watched her flow onto the top of a small desk with an easy grace envied by Helen's arthritic bones. Then, as Charlotte tried to return her smile, Helen saw that she had been crying.

"Can I help?" she asked.

Charlotte gave her another damp smile. "It's my evaluation. It didn't go well. Almada says I need to take some classes this summer in the Hunter teaching and learning concept. But I have to have a summer job, Helen, and Hunter isn't available in night classes."

"Dr. Hunter's theories are excellent, Charlotte. Can't you locate something you can work into your schedule?"

The girl shook her head. "Maybe I should just hang it up. I've had most of the proper courses and made good grades in them, but I'll never be the teacher you are, Helen."

"Nonsense!" Helen scoffed. "I've watched you, Charlotte. You have a special rapport with your second-graders." She stopped, surprised to discover that it was true. The little boys were "in love" with their pretty teacher, and the little girls tried to copy her.

"I was young once, believe it or not," she said, "and, like you, Charlotte, I was long on enthusiasm and short on experience. It will come with time. You will make a fine teacher. Don't give up!"

"I'm going to miss you, Helen," Charlotte said softly. "My mother deserted my father and me when I was six, and I haven't heard from her since. I have no living relatives, and I've always had more men than women friends." She paused. "What I'm trying to say, Helen, is I appreciate all you've done—attending my father's funeral when you hardly knew me, the birthday cake, the discipline tips. You've been like family to me, and I . . ." She looked away. "It . . . gets lonely sometimes."

Impulsively, Helen said, "I make a good pot of tea, Charlotte, if I do say so myself, and . . ." Suddenly, she had an inspiration. "Charlotte, I've had Hunter's training so many times, I practically know it by heart. And I have all the materials. You wouldn't get credit for it, of course, but I'd be glad to share it with you, any evenings you're free."

The girl's face brightened. "Oh, Miss Grace!" She slipped off the desk and stood in front of her. "You would do that for me?"

"I would enjoy it," Helen assured the girl. "Call me." She hesitated, swallowed hard, then said deliberately, "Call me Helen, Charlotte."

Her life was changing. There was no doubt about that, she thought, as she listened to Charlotte's heels click down the hall. She picked up her purse, walked to the door, then turned for one last look around the room.

She knew there would be times when she would long for the smell of chalk dust and Pine-Sol floor cleaner, for the sounds of rustling paper and scratching pencils. But retirement would allow her to do more of the counseling and remedial work she so often had wished she had time to provide. And she wouldn't have to quit working with a student just because he left fourth grade and became someone else's responsibility.

Shutting the door firmly behind her, Helen walked briskly down the hall and out the front door. On the front step, she paused and took a deep breath, catching a hint of freedom in the air, of new mission fields ripening in the early summer sun.

WANDA J. LUTTRELL is the author of many books and stories, the most recent being five Revolutionary War novels in the popular Sarah's Journey series, and *The Journey of Hannah*, of the Immigrants series, all published by Chariot Books. She and her husband have reared four daughters and a son just north of Frankfort, Kentucky, in a home they built in a wild, wooded meadow called (what else?) *Wildmeadow*. In her early years, she attended Bald Knob School, where her fourth-grade teacher was much like Helen Grace.

LEATRICE JOHNSON

Up from Bed

The gibbous moon shines
squares of light on my floor.
I know so few constellations
that, enlivening the night,
familiar Orion occupies the sky.
The three bright stars of his belt,
arms stretching the tight
string of his bow.
I push open the window,
and these stars do blink.
It's not just my eyes,
my unreliable eyes.
Orion rises, or more
rightly, I fall away,
and I think how these
stars shine,
tell me this old light
will pass over the small slice
of all I will ever know.
Awake,
I had failed to understand
how light travels.
But still drowsy,
it seems close to real,
how these stars may
already be dead
and dark and their
light still bends on.

LEATRICE JOHNSON lives and works in southern Vermont. She has been published in the *Midland Review* and Chrysalis Reader: *Decisions! Decisions!*.